The Orca Project~

A Meeting of
Nations

AN ANTHOLOGY

by Randall L. Eaton, P

SACRED PRESS

POST OFFICE BOX 490
ASHLAND, OREGON 97520

The Orca Project~

A Meeting of Nations

AN ANTHOLOGY

by Randall L. Eaton, Ph.D.

Published by
SACRED PRESS
POST OFFICE BOX 490
ASHLAND, OREGON 97520

-In Memory of-
James W. Foster, D.V. M.
-Friend and Mentor-

Please address inquiries to the author at:

Randall L. Eaton, Ph.D.

P.O. Box 490, Ashland, Oregon 97520

Library of Congress Catalog Card Number: 98-092-797

ISBN 0-966-3696-0-2

PRINTED AND BOUND IN THE UNITED STATES OF AMERICA

Cover painting by Jodi Bergsma

Cover & book design - WHITE SAGE STUDIOS
Drawer G, Virginia City, Nevada 89440

The Orca Project ~

A Meeting of
Nations
AN ANTHOLOGY

Books by Randall L. Eaton

The Cheetah: Biology, Behavior and Conservation of an Endangered Species

The Cheetah: Nature's Fastest Race

The World's Cats I: Ecology and Behavior (Editor)
The World's Cats II: Biology and Behavior of Reproduction (Editor)
The World's Cats III (1): Biology and Behavior (Editor)
The World's Cats III (2): Status, Management and Conservation (Editor)

The Status and Conservation of the Leopard in Sub-Saharan Africa

Marine Shoreland Fauna of Washington, Volumes I and II (Editor)

Zen and the Art of Hunting: A Personal Serarch for Environmental Values

My Animals, My Teachers

The Human/Animal Connection (Editor)

The Orca Project–A Meeting of Nations: An Anthology

The Sacred Hunt: An Anthology

A MEETING OF NATIONS:
for Nicola

by Randall L. Eaton

up north in B.C.
there's a killer whale named Nicola
for the nick in her dorsal fin

while we were sitting around the fire
talking about her kind
she surfaced ten feet off the point

without cameras
ten grownups ran to the post and yelled

    NICOLA
        NICOLA
            NICOLA

she hung on the surface out front
and called her clan together
daughters, nieces, grandaughters
in small delegations
swam in to check us out
spyhopping by the calves
screams and hoots by the humans
until all the orca young had seen us close up

the real work of whale watching
is the meeting of nations

Contents

1

Discovering the Orca

JIM AND JANE FOSTER AND I SAT TOGETHER and talked at their Lake Washington home. We were well into the second of our usual three glasses of wine when Jim's son, Jeff, phoned from the Seattle Aquarium and invited us down to the waterfront pier where they were preparing to load a large, female orca onto a boat bound for San Juan Island. The orca would be released into a cove and held temporarily there before reintroduced to Puget Sound.

On the way down I told Jim for the upteenth time my spiel about how orcas are the counterpart to man, the dominant, social predator of the marine world. Dominant until recently usurped by humanity that is. Though I had often thought about orcas and how they would provide the key to understanding human dominance and how we humans might better steward the world, I had never actually seen any except for Namu, years earlier when I first came to Seattle to start graduate school in zoology.

One of the first things I did in that fall of 1965 was go to the waterfront and watch Namu explode from Puget Sound with a full-grown man riding him. I knew enough then about animal behavior to know that it was quite remarkable that an adult, totally wild predator would become so tame and friendly to humans. The child of wonder inside me was so much in awe of him that, without intellectual musings, I knew that here was a marvelous, intelligent and incredibly sensitive and gentle being.

My life connected with orcas again three years later, oddly enough, at Purdue in northern Indiana. At our small field laboratory for animal behavior, which we had built on my professor's farm eight miles from Lafayette, were three men, and of them, my professor and fellow graduate student were the first behavioral scientists to systematically investigate the behavior of the orca. (Why, exactly, mid-westerners are pioneers in many fields is a subject we'll save for another place.) They went to Puget Sound and to the Johnstone Strait to observe them in the wild, and also visited oceanariums in Florida, California and the Pacific Northwest.

Rick had met our professor, Erik, at the University of Chicago where Rick had been a senior in Erik's animal behavior class. A city boy who had no special push in the direction of marine life or whales Rick had chosen to write his research paper on the orca, and after that he continued to conduct an independent research project that encompassed a massive, universal search of the literature. He even studied—Erik said he mastered—Japanese and Russian in order to read the many articles and notes containing information on orcas. Later when Rick joined Erik and me at the ethology laboratory, he picked up where he had left off and went with Erik to Seattle to conduct field work in 1969, the same year I departed for further investigation of African lion social behavior.

I had left Seattle in 1966 to undertake a study of the behavior and ecology of the cheetah in Kenya, after which my interests turned to the evolution of social behavior in the cat family, and from the cheetah, a semi-social species, to the extremely social lion. Which in turn led me to ideas about social evolution generally, and that back to a comparison of large, social carnivores, such as the wolf, hyena and lion, with humans and their evolutionary history. So, while doing post-doctoral research in feline behavior at Seattle's zoo and constructing grandiose theories about human origins, I was more receptive to the nature of the orca as a highly social, dominant predator with an extremely advanced brain. A great dolphin who ruled its world for millions of years, unlike humans who have been in charge for only a few hundred or thousand years on land, a few decades in the sea.

When we arrived at the Seattle Aquarium, what then was a private operation owned by Sea World, I recognized it to be where Namu had been exhibited as the first orca in captivity before he died. According to the trainers and aquarium personnel, Namu had drowned in the net. They said he was trying to join a wild female orca outside who had been visiting him for several days. They said that wild orcas whom they suspected of being members of Namu's society, had come to his net in the Sound off the end of the pier and interacted with him through the net. But, they added, after he'd been captive and alone for about a year, and the female orca who seemed to care so much for him returned to the net, one night he decided that he'd had enough. He was going to get free and rejoin the cow and wild orcas or die. He tried breaking through the net, they said, by hitting it head-first at the top speed he could muster within the confined area, but on his last effort he aimed at the lower part of the net, became wedged inside the hole he had made, and, unable to free himself, drowned.

Years later, the man who captured and rode Namu would tell a different story. Ted Griffin said in his 1982 book about Namu that the great orca had acquired a bacterial infection from the then polluted waters of Seattle's waterfront which killed him. We don't know which story to believe, if either. We came to believe over the years, however, that the certainly plausible portion of the first myth was that an orca could do such a thing as *knowingly* risk its life, even commit suicide. That

Griffin admits his knowledge of the possible risk of Seattle's sewage to Namu but did *not* do anything about it, such as move or sell Namu or release him, is bad enough; that he brought in more orcas to the same, polluted environment that killed Namu is sad.

Almost ten years after Namu died and I left Seattle for Africa, there I was again with the first orcas to attract so much attention since Namu. The year was 1976, and at that time in Seattle, which is the world's most environmentally conscious city with the highest level of education per capita, the uproar may have been expected. The newspapers, TV stations and radio had been focusing on the capture of orcas for weeks. Nobody was unaware of the controversy and most people had strong opinions in the matter. Since Ted Griffin had "captured" Namu in British Columbia, half of the orcas that ended up in aquariums around the world, from Japan to South Africa and San Diego to Holland, had been captured in Puget Sound. The people of Seattle had had enough. Fomented by the radical students, eco-freaks and whale hippies from Evergreen State College sixty miles away at the southernmost tip of Puget Sound, people were turning out by the thousands to protest the capture of more orcas for Sea World. Besides having dramatically altered local, regional and world perception of orcas, which, in 1965 were still being shot for bounty paid by the Washington Department of Game, Namu's tenure in Seattle may be held as the primary influence behind public concern for protecting Puget Sound's wild orcas from any form of exploitation. In merely a decade the orca had moved from being a feared, persecuted creature to a revered being.

Some Nasty Rumors

The Evergreen College whale people had spread far and wide some nasty rumors, press releases and documentation to the effect that the Puget Sound orca population could be declining seriously as a direct result of ten years of captures. Evergreen being the state's alternative college with a heavy emphasis on environmental and marine studies and a policy that sends students into the "real world" to conduct research projects and gain first-hand knowledge of subjects, some of the last hippies had been working intensely in orca studies for private whale-watching groups and state agencies. They had uncovered the unsavory details: about sixty had died during capture or been removed from an original population of perhaps a hundred and fifty.

Orcas are not highly fecund. They give birth to one offspring at a time at a maximum rate of one every four or five years, and an orca may not reproduce until well after its fifteenth year. As high-ranking carnivores who weigh several tons each, their food and range requirements are very large. As a species that is highly social it is conceivable that all the deaths and removals of orcas did depress the resident population of Puget Sound to the point of a critical threshold from which they might not be able to recover. (For example, in 1985, K-pod had its first birth in ten years.) Even the resource managers had to admit this possibility. But not only were the media passing on the idea that many of Puget Sound's orcas were already gone, they were suggesting the most unpopular allegation that in the course of ten years of captures many orcas had been killed, some even had been sunken by the capture team to hide the evidence of deaths occuring during capture, something I was able to confirm and document over time.

The Evergreen people were arguing that the capture efforts alone could be harmful or lethal to orcas, and if not that, socially disruptive, which could indirectly be lethal. The students and their sympathizers took to Greenpeace tactics intended to stop the capture. They went so far, as one of them admitted to me later, to sneak up on the orcas inside nets floating in the Sound, dive underwater in the dark and cut the nets. Public concern mounted all the way to Washington, D. C., where Washington's senior senator, Warren Magnuson, then reputed to be the most powerful member of the U.S. Senate, responded by having Puget Sound declared a federally protected area for marine mammals. Seattle's totem creature, emblazened on restaurant walls and in thousands of dens in the style of the Northwest Coastal Indians, who revere the orca, had received a sanctuary.

A federal judge demanded the release of all but two whales which could be used temporarily only for research in Puget Sound. The orcas were entrusted to a local research professor at the University of Washington's College of Fisheries, who received a grant of about $30,000 for a pilot study on the feasibility of radio-tracking the movements of free-swimming orcas. The orcas were to be held in a naturalistic setting for about a month then released with radio-transmitters secured to their bodies which would allow the scientist to monitor the orcas' movements.

What I saw two orcas do that evening in the small holding pool at the end of the pier changed my life and started me on my most adventurous experience in animal behavior, the discovery of what these pages testify to be extra-terrestrial, intelligent life, possibly with answers to humanity's global crisis. Amidst the confusion of seventy people including divers, TV cameramen, aquarium staff and assorted guests, the orcas swam in circles around the shallow pool where they had been placed after being captured to prevent anyone from releasing them. For several days the orcas had been in a pool, scarcely longer than the adult female, with a pair of small porpoises. To aquarium visitors, this datum might have seemed less than significant; many people have seen orcas and dolphins performing together, but for me, a student of the behavior of large carnivores, here was a most unexpected phenomenon. Unlike all other orcas in captivity these two orcas were the "transient" type, i.e., predators of mammals.

Imagine for a moment what might occur if a mature, wild lion were placed into a cage for a week with a pair of impalas. It's true that a wild lion might not attack its natural prey initially, at least not while humans were present or until it had explored its confined environment, but if left alone with antelope for very long the outcome would be certain—it would kill and eat them. Even a captive-born lion without any predatory experience will attack and maul its natural prey under these circumstances; I know because I have observed it happen. Why I'd never pondered how it was possible for wild-caught orcas to be kept with dolphins in aquariums without the dolphins being eaten I can't say. Like everyone else who had seen the orca/dolphin shows I never paused to wonder about these species' unlikely relationship in captivity. Instead, I was one who was always reminding people that not only will lions kill cheetahs, feline against feline, they will certainly kill, even eat, other lions.

From reading I believed then that all orcas prefer mammalian prey, including dolphins, members of their family, not their species, and other whales, which is how they received the name "killer whale," which, in the original was "whale killer," killer of whales, not humans. Killer whale is a tragic misnomer, an accident of translation which has cost many orcas their lives precisely because humans use the word killer as an adjective to describe any animal that threatens or kills them. Anyone who has watched old cowboy films or television for very long has encountered terms such as "killer cat" or "killer bear" for beasts who supposedly have killed people. Dubbed as the "killer" whale, orcas have been shot by the hundreds because men assumed from the name itself that they are dangerous, best gotten rid of if possible. And this sad scenario also points to the manner in which humans gained dominance over all other lifeforms—not merely by hunting but by outcompeting other predators, the first and oldest form of human warfare.

Now classic experiments document without doubt that natural enemies may live peacefully together *if* humans manipulate their early developmental experience. Housecats raised with rats or mice won't attack them as adults. To the cat, the rat is essentially something other than prey. Whether a cat raised with rats perceives the rats as the same as cats seems unlikely, but surely they are not what a cat should attack for food. The cat has been socialized to rats because the cat's knowledge about what is its own species is determined by the parent or siblings it grows up with…normally mother cats and other kittens. When we alter things by taking advantage of the cat's instinctive tendency to identify its species in early experience, part of "being my species" means to the cat that it is inhibited about perceiving its "pseudo-sibling" rats as prey.

Whether this experiment is conducted with lions and sheep or bears and deer or dogs and cats, the species that are enemies in nature become tame and friendly to one another throughout their lives. But when orcas have been observed to catch and eat porpoises in Puget Sound, and then are put into an environment in which they could easily chomp them, behavioral science offers no explanation for why they don't. Perhaps it's been far easier to ignore such exceptions, limited, as far as I know, to cetaceans. The worst aspect of science is that it pretends that glaring exceptions are insignificant when history shows that human ideas grow precisely as a result of redefining theories to accommodate exceptions.

Orca Helps Dolphin Give Birth

As a matter of record, *Pacific Search* magazine, headquartered in Seattle, published photos of an adult female orca, Skana, helping a Pacific white-sided dolphin deliver her baby. The process is the same for both orcas and dolphins in which other females of a social group lend aid by lifting the newborn to the surface for air, but this common pattern hardly accounts for interspecies cooperation. By everything I thought I knew before standing in front of two orcas with two porpoises passing inches from the orcas' jaws time and again, I never would have predicted that orcas would help dolphins give birth in an aquarium. One would be equally surprised, really, that the dolphin would permit it. Why wouldn't she be terribly upset over a giant orca placing its jaws on her baby?

Yet, both parties conducted themselves with no indication of anything but complete cooperation and trust.

Despite the scientific doctrine of anthropomorphism, which has dulled Occam's razor and made it useless, science is a matter of discovering "the pattern that connects," as Gregory Bateson said. As we overview the behavior of humans and non-humans there is a pattern that connects orca behavior to that of humans. I could easily imagine that a human placed into captivity might much prefer living there in the presence of another species which had been its prey. If I were locked into a zoo or prison cage with a deer as my sole companion, even though I had hunted and eaten deer regularly, I think I would eat frozen zupreem—a commercial diet for zoo carnivores, which, judging by their response to it, would be less than appetizing—and let the deer survive. A lion would not do that; neither would a wild, adult wolf or bear, but at least some humans would just to make their life more interesting, less boring. *Decidedly anthropomorphic, this idea necessarily presupposes that orcas are comparable to humans in so far as they are capable of adjusting their behavior, consciously and deliberately, according to a conceptual analysis of the costs and benefits involved over the long haul.* It would mean, of course, that the transient orcas removed from Puget Sound and put with dolphins comprehended that they were being held captive along with the dolphins, and, perhaps, that in the face of an unrelated, dominant species, they should hold back eating the dolphins in favor of the possibility that cooperation with them could prove more adaptive in the end. However we interpret their behavior, anthropomophizing is inescapable for a freely thinking person confronted with the bizarre behavior of orcas and dolphins, and in itself, that is a scientific and human revolution.

Do Orcas Empathize with Captive Dolphins?

Actually, the comparison I drew between a captivated human and orcas does not give justice to the orcas. In the hypothetical human case, I proposed that the person would be alone except for a deer, but I did not mention that the female orca that volunteered to nursemaid the dolphin was *not* alone but living with another orca. This fact engenders thoughts of a wholly different level of explanation: perhaps orcas *empathize* with dolphins in captivity, in which case their sophisticated transformation from dolphin-predator to dolphin-helper is no self-serving thing but as moral as the highest human morality, selfless love, what the original Roman philosophers of Christianity termed universal benevolence, not simply to humankind but to all creatures.

My mind reeled with the tension of reluctance as I reached beyond the accepted doctrines of animal behavior to explain the sight of wild predators relating harmoniously with their natural prey. That was but the first sample of how orcas would twist my thoughts around and bring me into confrontation with myself and my world. In short, I was beginning a personal revolution.

The water level in the tank was dropping. Jeff and some other young men were pulling on wet suits before entering the pool. The female orca appeared to be fully adult; she was several feet longer and heavier than the male. Her behavior under the circumstances indicated that she may have been the male's mother or aunt, and in any case, they came from the same society which meant they probably were close relatives. As the orcas continued to circle counter-clockwise, the female was in the lead, the male always right behind, his head almost touching her fluke. Several times as they passed Jim and me, the young male opened his jaws and raised his head slightly, pointing his gaping mouth at us. Jim figured that this was a kind of threat gesture, which was right, and I reckoned that the male threatened us because we were by far the most intent observers around the tank. Staring or prolonged eye contact is threatening in every species for which vision is an important sense, and as intent observers, Jim and I were eliciting threat-gapes from the male.

As the water level dropped lower, the crane from the boat was swung overhead. The cable held a loose canvas sling that was to be used to lift the female out of the pool onto the back of the boat. The male would be moved separately after the female was carried north and released in the island cove. As the water reached a level where the adult female could barely move without touching the bottom with her pectoral fins and fluke, she turned around to face the young male and made some audible sounds, apparently directed at him. Immediately he altered his behavior by positioning himself in the corner of the tank opposite from where the canvass would be lowered. He began a series of repetitive behavior: he inhaled what seemed to be a great volume of air, closed his blow-hole tight, then sank to the tank floor, leaving perhaps a foot of water covering all but his dorsal fin. While resting there on the bottom he slowly exhaled air, which made a gurgling sound. Normally, orcas expel air all at once in a virtual explosion at the surface, or in small trickles underwater when they produce complex sounds believed to be communicative—not merely sonar blasts.

Here was my first insight into orca communication. The adult female had communicated something to the effect that the young male should remain in the corner and spend as much time as possible underwater, apparently for protection. The strange gurgling behavior of the submerged whale was no accident, but apparently a form of communication that signalled continually that he was situated in very shallow water. When orcas hunt seals, they often swim in the shallow surf and they may even leap out of the water onto the shore to grab a victim. The risk of being stranded in shallow water or on shore is high for any cetacean, and the young male was producing sounds underwater that an orca would unintentionally make if it were breathing in water the depth of its blow-hole. Perhaps all young orcas automatically produce the "gurgling" call whenever they encounter shallows.

The female continued swimming in circles, and twice when the young male started to follow her as she passed his corner position, she wheeled around to face him, made more sounds and actually struck him, once with an upward jerk of her head against his thorax, another time with a blow from her pectoral fin. She seemed to be scolding him and insisting that he stay put there and not follow her. The orcas had been moved from a net in the Sound to the pool on the pier with the same boat crane and canvas lift which had been swung into place above the pool when she first forced him into a less conspicuous and inactive posture. She may have recognized the danger at hand—being lifted out of the water must be very disturbing to an orca, rather like being forced underwater might seem to a human—and was trying to protect the male.

When the water dropped so low that the female could barely move through it, the divers stepped into the water which came up to their waists.

Though I had seen humans cavorting with orcas in seaquariums, here I was witnessing the unexpected again: puny, unprotected humans moving around among two of the world's most awesome marine predators, and they took no precautions whatsoever. The orcas were motionless in the water, their heads oriented to and tracking the divers who were guiding the canvas lift into place at the end of the pool next to Jim and me. Several times a diver walked alongside the female and touched her body with his hands but she didn't respond. I became nervous when Jeff stood for some time right in front of the female's mouth. Easily she could have grabbed him in her jaws and literally cut him in two with a single bite, but she didn't even open her jaws to threaten him.

I shook my head sideways and mumbled to Jim, "Incredible, absolutely incredible. Imagine what would happen, Jim, if these orcas were wild lions or grizzly bears right about now. Jeff's life would be in danger, but look at this. Its incredible and I don't know what to make of it." Jim assured me I had nothing to fear, that this was the way it had always been between men and orcas during capture and afterwards in holding pools or the orcas' new home in captivity. Ample proof was before us. We agreed that the female's interactions with the male indicated her fear of the lift and her protectiveness of the male, but that being the case, why wasn't she aggressively defensive, if not of herself then the male, once the divers entered the pool?

My questions could not keep pace with events. As the crane lowered the lift into place and a diver unfolded the canvas and spread it out across the bottom of the pool, the female positioned herself behind it as though expecting something. Jim explained to me that they would try to entice her over the canvas and then wrap it around her and lift her out and onto the back of the boat. How, I was curious, do you move a wild predator of several tons over the spot where you want it and then hold it in place? How many divers would have to risk their lives to budge a reluctant sea monster into a contraption that already surely has terrified it?

You don't do any of that. Such tactics would be too dangerous even if they could work. You leave it up to the orca to do what you could not possibly force it to do. The female put herself in precisely the proper position over the canvas. No one guided her or enticed her or frightened her into place. She simply did it herself. Now I was beside myself, flabbergasted and confused. This creature belonged to a highly social species of dominant predator but it was very different than a lion or wolf, and I am not sure that captured humans of an alien culture would be so cooperative with their captors. It is one thing to say we understand why a mother or aunt might offer herself up to captors as a means of protecting a son or nephew, but with such apparent fearlessness and directness of purpose? To be removed from one's water world?

The divers secured the loose end of the canvas around her body by hooking it over the steel pole hanging from the cable. The motor operating the cable began to whine as the female lifted slowly off the bottom. The scene everyone had worked so hard to create was passing amid silence and wonder save that of the winch and the clicks of cameras. When the female was about six feet above the water the cable snapped and she fell with a thud against the floor of the tank. The abdomen of orcas is soft, unprotected by bone and poorly adapted to withstand the impact of several tons striking a solid substrate. The fall could have seriously injured her, were it not for the cushion of water; however, judging by her behavior she was frightened and possibly hurt. For about thirty minutes she thrashed around the pool as though in protest, and when the young male seemed to want to leave his post and join her, she clobbered him with a stiff jab of her head to his body.

If everything that had already transpired were not enough to firmly impress me with the unexpected behavior of orcas, what occurred next did. After the female calmed down, the cable was repaired and the lift was lowered again. The divers spread the canvas out as before, and though the female wasn't completely voluntary in placing herself in proper position, she responded to the gentle tugging of divers' hands and moved into place. I could not imagine any animal or human in a comparable situation effectively submitting to being lifted a second time after being dropped the first. She did. There was no accident as she was lowered onto the boat which chugged through the night towards San Juan Island. Once on the boat the female began to scream and cry—the best short-hand descriptions of the sound she made—all the way to the island.

Jim introduced me to the scientist in charge of the project. I told him that I would volunteer my services as behaviorist. He had no one in mind and felt that he could use me so I left the aquarium to get my sound recording gear and cameras together for an over-night trip by road and ferry to San Juan Island. I wanted to be there in the morning when the female arrived and was released in the cove.

2

Communicating with Orcas

THE TRAILER AT THE HEAD OF KANAKA BAY provided protection from the rain and wind of March. An undergraduate student named Brad and an employee of Sea World-San Diego, John Colby, were there waiting before sunrise for the boat to arrive. We sat and drank coffee from thermoses and talked about the project. John filled me in on the direction of the research and the ground rules that had been established by the scientist in charge, Al Erickson. It was not precisely clear why Sea World was still involved with the orcas or why Don Goldsberry, who had captured the orcas, was an unofficial boss here. Perhaps Colby and Goldsberry were loaned to the orca-tracking project to boost Sea World's image after devastating press coverage of the protest over its capture of orcas.

After explaining to them that I'd be there most of the time for the next month, and that when I wasn't, my students would be, John said he'd make arrangements with the owner of the land around the cove to let me stay in the rough hewn cabin. The owner was one of my colleagues in the zoology department in Seattle, however, neither as a graduate student in the mid-60s nor as a faculty member in the mid-70s had I ever met the man.

The boat arrived in the cove as the sun was rising. Jeff and two other divers went into the water inside the net which John had rigged across the mouth of the cove. The crane hoisted the orca over the net and into the water as the divers unfastened the canvas to free her. As I sat on the bank overlooking the cove and filmed, again I was impressed with the astounding lack of aggression from the orca. She could have killed all three of the divers in seconds, but there was not as much as a fluke slap or gape. The orca swam underwater in the deep end of the cove as the boat departed for Seattle and the male it would deliver next.

Studying animal behavior is a human enterprise that pre-dates anything else that may properly be termed human. The long journey of our ancestors was begun with the alertness, attentiveness and imitation of animals required of a primate predator, and over evolutionary time, the motivation, basic skills and built-in reinforcers for studying animal behavior acquired a life of their own, irrespective of hunting itself. My relationship to the orcas was one of a silent observer who sat for eighteen hours a day noting their every gesture, interaction, blow and sound. My shelf has a notebook of over 200 typed pages—description of two orcas' behavior during a month's captivity in the cove.

With the aid of a hydrophone and a reel-to-reel tape recorder left by an Evergreen College student, I was able to lis-ten in on the orcas' vocal exchanges and correlate their sound communication with their behavior and circumstances. I was not there to intrude or intervene, as did John Colby, who wast-ed hundreds of pounds of frozen herring trying to get the orcas to eat. They wouldn't, and within a few days we had hundreds of gulls flying in to grab the fish. I wasn't there to make period-ic measurements of how long the orcas take between blows, Erickson's instructions to Brad which he hoped would indicate how often and for how long orcas came up out of the water to breath. Only then would the radios transmit sound which could be received and monitored to get bearings on their location and direction of movement after released from the cove.

My observations continued largely unabated despite the comings and goings of the press, confrontations with trespassers who were angry at us for containing the orcas, well wishers who came to admire and photograph the orcas, and, of course, bureaucrats galore. After the big fuss over the orcas in Seattle, the good public servants had to visit the cove before they'd put a stamp of approval on the project. Al spent most of the month flying back and forth in float planes with TV crews and dignitaries. The state game and fisheries personnel and federal officials came and left in droves. An enforcement officer of the National Marine Fisheries Service declared, "If you ask me, they're just a big fish, that's all." I couldn't pretend to be amused.

Early in the study I discovered that the orcas could hear float planes coming long before any of us could see or hear them. Sound travels more than three times faster underwater than it does in air, and several minutes before we sensed an approaching plane the orcas gave it away by diving deep and circling underwater for long periods between blows. They seemed to be frightened of the sound of float planes, which had been used to drop bombs and to scare them into a cove where they were netted.

It became obvious, too, that the female always made the same, specific sound, echoed by the young male, just before they both dived and stayed submerged in advance of a plane's arrival. The "vocabulary" of orca sounds was complex, varied and efficient. A few calls were not difficult to decipher; at least some of the meaning was clear. The greeting call, for example, was easily recognized, as was the "float plane alarm" call.

Though it was believed by Colby that orcas may go months without eating because they supposedly lay on so much fat during part of the year that they don't need to eat during the rest, the male was young and growing, probably in need of food. John thought his dorsal fin was drooping too much. The fin is composed largely of cartilage and adipose tissue, and John was concerned that the drooping of the fin indicated a loss of fat stores. But the orcas wouldn't touch the frozen herring. We tried negotiating a deal for live fish with the Lummi Indians who were culturing salmon. Though salmon could swim through the holes in the net, the orcas would probably catch a few first, we hoped; however, the Lummis wanted too much money for the fish. Then Jerry Brown volunteered his expert diving ability, and brought in a small sea bass which he had speared in the tail without killing it.

I tied the fish on the line of my spinning rod, and John lowered the fish into the cove. The male oriented to the bass, emitted a sonar blast, swam to it, and when inches away, opened his mouth. We were excited because it appeared that the male would eat live fish one at a time, which meant we could prevent him from starving. With his jaws ready to close over the bass, the male stopped, backed away from the bass and swam off. The female had been observing the entire affair, and, she too, had emitted a sonar click in the direction of the fish when it was lowered into the water. From half way across the cove she emitted a second sound as she faced the male who had his mouth open to bite the fish, and that seemed to account for his sudden change of mood. Contained within this particular sound, which I hadn't recorded earlier, was a message to stop, "Don't eat that fish."

As though to accentuate or punctuate her command to the male, the female then swam back and forth between us and the male slapping her fluke on the water. Fluke lobbing is often associated with behavior and contexts that suggest it is a warning.

Though the male acted as though he wanted to eat the sea bass, he ignored it once the female warned him. Perhaps she had sensed the fine line, merely 4-pound monofilament, attached to the fish's gills. Orcas catch salmon, and many salmon carry lures and plugs with hooks and lines trailing from their mouths, so perhaps it was the fishing line that prompted her to warn the male. To test this idea we released the sea bass from the fishing line, but the orcas ignored it. Perhaps it wasn't the fishing line at all but the female's awareness that we were offering the fish—maybe she didn't trust us.

Whenever visitors appeared on the horizon above the cove, the orcas habitually dived and stayed down until they left. I was certain that the orcas heard air-borne sound quite a distance from the water, since, as with the float planes, their behavior often cued me to people approaching before I heard or saw them.

One quiet, sunny afternoon I found myself alone again on the rocky cliff above the cove where the female often stayed. For three weeks I had sat there listening and recording, filming and taking notes, without interacting directly with the orcas. I wanted to swim with them and had asked Jeff to bring Jim's wet suit in case Al would consent to my entering the water. The orcas must have been curious about me, too, because what occurred next catapulted me into a new level of relationship with orcas and all things wild.

For thousands of circles the orcas had come around below the rocks where I sat, but this time their behavior was very different, conspicuously slow, so slow in fact that I barely discerned forward movement. With the female in the lead, as usual, both orcas turned their heads sideways about thirty degrees which brought their eyes above water, and as they passed by only a few feet away at the peak of the high tide, they looked straight into my eyes. Neither orca had exhibited any similar behavior to anyone or anything throughout the study, but there they were observing and inspecting me carefully.

Then it happened. Somehow by means other than normal sensory communication the orcas communicated to me, "We know what you're doing, and it's all right." Literally, I fell over backwards, stunned by their psychic communication. Now, I had *never* expected, anticipated or thought about psychic communication with orcas or any other non-human; I had never taken LSD or read a single book by John Lilly, not even his books about dolphins; and, in short, I was neither a "whale hippy" nor a scientist who, until then, had anticipated being able to write something like this even if it had occurred. My questions were fundamentally sound, and by no one's standards unconventional or implausible. In one unexpected moment, a person whose world did not encompass psychic communication with non-humans was irrevocably transformed. It was something I could not possibly turn my back on because "there's no way to test" it. I knew what I had to do.

The day of the low, low tide had come. Al would be able to beach the orcas, and surgically install the radio transmitter on the male and inspect the female's radio. A retinue of divers, marine mammal veterinarians, and documentary photographers converged on the cove.

The opportunity to collect specimens from living, untamed orcas was not to be refused—scientific trophies in the offing. My students and I would never have conceived or approved of what was planned for that morning, and though we did not directly participate, we observed and documented on film and taped the proceedings.

The male orca rested on the bottom in eighteen inches of water, encircled by men in blue and black wet suits. A drill bored holes through his dorsal fin where surgical bolts would hold fast the radio transmitter pack. It won't hurt him, they'd proclaimed confidently, smugly, because, they insisted, the fin is mostly fatty tissue. The sounds on the tapes we collected that morning say otherwise. I have played them to people who knew nothing about the origin or context of the sounds, and, invariably, they describe them as someone screaming. The male orca was capable enough even while partially stranded to strike out with his jaws or body to defend himself against what could be interpreted only as extremely painful but simply cried out. The pathetic sounds bear no resemblance to the usual phonations of orcas, and their ability to evoke from humans the interpretation of "someone screaming in pain"or "somebody crying for help" cannot be taken lightly. The female orca's extremely agitated response to the male's horrible cries further corroborated our own emotional response.

Then the veterinarian pushed large-bore needles eight inches into the orca's flesh to "collect blood and tissue samples" for further analyses, and, again, the poor orca screamed. To this day, unfortunately, one may enter into fruitless arguments about whether orcas, dolphins or whales feel pain. The most innervated skin known to science must be, for a yet unidentified reason, insensitive to pain.

After the orcas were released, they disappeared. By all appearances their response to being tracked was a clever, sophisticated and quite deliberate escape strategy. Their escape was made good by forcing the trackers to choose to follow one of them. The mirror image routes they employed transcribed what many people, including more open-minded scientists, figured to be an optimal pattern for escape.

Later when I ran into Brad on Orcas Island where he was looking for the orcas, he was no longer smug, and there seemed to be a sign of humility about him. The orcas had impressed him with their ability to elude humans in boats and planes. In any case, Brad had not seen hide nor fin of "U.S. 1" or "U.S. 2," labels Erickson tattooed on the orcas' fins and painted on their transmitter packs to make sure that any Canadian biologists would know to whom the orcas rightfully belonged. Erickson's great plans for attracting a sizable grant to track orcas fell through. The orcas relocated their society in British Columbia, and twenty years later one of them is easily recognized by the holes in its fin where the radio had been fixed.

Several months after completing the observations in the cove on San Juan Island, Kelly Noble and I used a sonograph to convert our tape recordings of the orca's phonations in the cove into sonograms, pictures of sound which depict intensity or amplitude, duration and frequency or pitch. Then I went to a friend who worked full-time for the Navy as a computer linguist while pursuing a graduate degree in Classics after having received degrees in mathematics and German. Hanus decided that the best approach to the question of language would be to sort each sonogram according to its structure. Independently, we sorted the sonograms made from the first 160 recorded sounds into the same categories without exception, and that assured me that our criteria for categorizing sonograms was valid.

When we finished, we had identified sixty-five distinct phonemes among the 160 sonograms. If the orcas' sounds represent language—they may represent something far more advanced than language—then their vocabulary is slightly higher than that of English. In other words, the sounds that orcas make are more diverse than those of English. And if they are not language then the very least that may be said is that orcas use a much greater expression of sounds than heretofore imagined for any non-human mammal. Thirty separate calls is the maximum found among advanced mammals including primates, but we discovered sixty-five distinct calls in the first 160 samples.

Whatever orcas are doing with sound, no one may deny that they are communicating, and no one may deny that their use of sound is highly developed and complex, enough to warrant linguistic analyses.

But the matter is yet more complicated. Three years after the Kanaka Bay study, we collected sound recordings at Victoria's Sea Land Aquarium which covered the full spectrum of orca sounds. Orcas produce sounds that extend up to about 250,000 cycles per second or about ten times more range than what most humans hear; orcas have the broadest spectrum of sound production known for any species in the world, including other members of the dolphin family. With the normal tape recorder, one may record sounds up to about 25,000 cycles per second, but with the cooperation and assistance of the Applied Physics Laboratory at the University of Washington, a leading center for study of submarine sonar and

Bull orca in Johnstone Strait, British Columbia.

detection, we were able to use a portable tape recorder worth over fifty thousand dollars to record orca sounds.

At the Physics Lab we listened to the same sounds broadcast over twelve separate channels, each one representing a frequency spectrum of about 20,000 cycles. The technician slowed down each segment to our hearing range and, much to my surprise, we learned that the same, brief sound we normally heard and recorded varied enormously in quality as the frequency bands increased. That is, what sounded to us at the moment of recording to be the "squeaky door" call sounded like several different calls as we listened to the higher frequency elements accompanying that sound. One orca sound is actually many different sounds packed into a highly energetic, incredibly brief emission. The ultra-sounds were not the same as audible sounds, which means that the orca's "vocabulary" may be far more complicated than human language. What all might an orca communicate in less than a second?

3

A Most Unusual Welcome

HAVING BECOME ENRAPTURED WITH ORCAS, I was elated to be visiting an aquarium with them. As I entered Sea Land of Victoria the young adult male, Haida, was at the shallow end of his pool opening his mouth on command to display fifty conical teeth to the hundreds of tourists crowded around. Haida's trainer was befuddled when Haida broke out of his well established opening routine to swim directly off to the side of the pool where I had squeezed in between two people. I was sure that he had singled me out of the audience, though exactly how was unclear since he had not been looking in my direction, and I had made no unusual movements or sounds.

Haida came up immediately in front of me and sprayed a fine fountain of water through his teeth over my head and the movie camera I was operating. The trainer was standing up by now and muttering, and later when we talked he assured me that he'd never seen Haida break his routine or squirt a tourist except on command. Unlike many dolphin and orca trainers, and other "animal men" generally, he held tremendous respect

Bull orca with Orca Project voulunteers off San Juan Island.

for the intelligence and awareness of these animals, and this was clearly shown in his rapport with them. So, when I explained to him that I held orcas in high esteem. and had shared what essentially were psychic communications with them which amounted to no less than a religious experience for me, he wasn't surprised at Haida's exceptional greeting. His warmth indicated what both of us felt for the orca—awe—and communicated without words an understanding, which, though ineffable, may be described as immodest humility. Our common connection made of us kindred spirits.

Our students spent months filming, recording and observing Haida, and among other fascinating things, we learned that his trainer didn't actually train him, at least not in the usual sense of behavioral psychology. Whenever the trainer wanted Haida to perform a *new* movement he simply gave him a hand signal to which Haida responded by inventing behavior patterns, none of which he had exhibited before and many of which had never been recorded in nature or captivity. Here was a most remarkable instance of meta-communication between man and orca. The message was not to do this or that as indicated by application of reinforcement following the desirable behavior, but rather, do something new and different—create! When the trainer observed a new behavior that he liked he simply gestured with another hand signal that said. "That one. Adopt that behavior into your routine," and Haida did. So very incredibly did this relationship evidence the highly evolved cognitive faculty of the orca that we carefully documented it on film.

Like many orcas in captivity, Haida had a mind of his own, as the trainers say. While dolphins almost always perform on command, orcas have a widespread reputation among the men and women who "train" them for becoming "moody" and refusing to perform, sometimes for months during which they are deprived of food or attention. Considering the horrible manner in which nearly every captive orca has been kept, deprived of sufficient social interaction and a level of activity appropriate to their needs, their apparent protests are not to be unexpected. That equally deprived dolphins do not seem to go on strike for better living conditions says something about the difference between them and orcas, which, after all are heir to the kingdom of the sea, a position of no small significance.

Both dolphins and the orca, largest member of the dolphin family, are quite intelligent. They learn quickly, as quickly as humans according to scientific investigation, but only the orca is apt to disobey. In training dolphins, pilot whales and orcas, the Navy achieved similar results from these species in performing various tasks on command. Equally well prepared to retrieve objects at sea, the dolphins and pilot whales performed admirably, but not the orca. Sent to pick up and return a submerged object, the orca dived alright but it just kept on swimming. What might we expect from the ruler of its world?

Two years after we last saw Haida, Sea Land was planning to release him into the sea. He had lived in captivity longer than any orca, and for most of that time he was isolated from other orcas. He had his moody periods, and by every measure, suffered from boredom; nonetheless, Haida had fared longer if not better than most. The strangest thing happened the day before his much publicized release: he drowned in his own pool. One Sea Land employee reported that Haida drowned himself, though the management concocted some story about a bacterial infection, as unsatisfactory an explanation for drowning as one of the more common excuses for why orcas die in captivity, "brain damage."

The puzzle remains why Haida died, and if he did commit

suicide, which seems indisputable for orcas during capture efforts in Puget Sound, why did he?

Is it possible, and in light of orca behavior, plausible, that Haida knew what humans had planned for him, but decided that he should die there at Sea Land? Did he fear his freedom perhaps? Or, feeling that his goodwill ambassadorship to humanity was finished, and mission accomplished, did he choose to die? Possibly, Haida felt rejected by his surrogate society and wanted to make a symbolic gesture with his death, a message that he preferred to remain where he was but in light of his keepers' inability to fathom his wishes he would drown himself to wake us up? None of these speculations are beyond the realm of possibility for two reasons: first, we are dealing with an extremely intelligent, highly evolved organism with a more developed ethical nature than ourselves; and, second, all hypotheses begin as speculations which are essentially projections of the human mind, in this case, how or why we might behave as Haida did under his circumstances. That many scientists will condemn me for publicizing my thoughts not only proves that freedom of thought is vastly discouraged in science, I dare say that it points to the glaring fact that we very much need to wake up.

I do *not* know why Haida drowned, and I have not said that he committed suicide, though certainly he may have...based on evidence of apparent suicides by orcas elsewhere. But I am saying that there is absolutely no reason to continue imagining that only humans are capable of suicide. The arrogant human mentality works something like this at best: Though we can understand why a human in comparable circumstances as Haida might commit suicide—rejection, fear of the wilderness, etc. —Haida was not human, therefore the hypothesis that he did commit suicide is invalid, and besides, there is no way he could have known that they were planning to release him. How could he have? He's only an animal, and you can't expect anyone to believe that he could perceive the intentions of Sea Land. End of inquiry. Humans, 1, orcas. 0.

4

Lessons From
White Wing and Skana

TONI AND I HAD BEEN COMING with the students to observe and film orca behavior in the show pool at Vancouver Aquarium, and today was our first behind the scenes trip. The management agreed to let us come in at eight a.m. when the feeders and trainers arrived, and observe the orcas and dolphin until ten a.m., opening hour. Of course, we had received strict instructions, and we adhered to them.

White Wing was a small dolphin who performed several times a day with the orcas. She spent the evening and early morning in the small pool adjacent to the show pool with a young adult orca, Hyak. The mature female orca, Skana, spent the evening alone in the show pool. As six of us gathered around the pool containing White Wing, she moved from person to person, making eye contact, gesturing with her rostrum, opening her jaws and squeaking. Everyone of us watched one of the aquarium employees reach down and touch White Wing on the head, and each of us hoped to be able to do the same.

White Wing came up out of the water in front of Toni,

but just as Toni's open hand was to contact White Wing, Toni experienced momentary fright at the sight of the dolphin's open mouth and teeth. Her fingers drew up into a fist, and White Wing snapped her. I was next, and as White Wing came up to greet me I was not afraid of being bitten so she gently closed her mouth on my open hand. And then I caressed her head.

I took the opportunity to point out to the students that the world often will oblige us, that our expectations influence our behavior and therefore the response of other creatures to us. In this case of White Wing snapping Toni's hand, Toni had communicated her fear to White Wing, and White Wing had communicated back to Toni a message that could be interpreted two ways: a) White Wing doesn't like you; or, b) White Wing doesn't like you to be afraid. The former assessment would only confirm Toni's fear of being bitten by a dolphin, a self-fulfilling prophesy, but the latter would lead to an awareness that dolphins are extremely perceptive.

I added that if White Wing had really wanted to hurt Toni, she could have very easily, but her bite brought no blood. It was more like a scolding. Confirmation was in order so I asked Toni to relax, to reach out to White Wing just as she had done before but without any fear and apprehension. I reminded her that White Wing meant no harm and that if she would simply trust White Wing and follow her affection then White Wing would respond accordingly. Surely Toni believed all this after having watched the rest of us touch White Wing without being snapped. Toni reached down over the edge of the pool and, as expected, White Wing came up, and let Toni pet her this time.

Tom wanted to know more about the perceptual capacities of dolphins and orcas: could they perceive human intentions directly without their ordinary senses or did they possess extra sensory perception? The students had been studying sonar and they had a real appreciation of just how very sophisticated communication is in some cetaceans. We discussed the possibility that before sonar was discovered, a naturalist observing dolphins easily might have suspected that they communicated or detected things by e.s.p., the point being that what we now term extra sensory may not be that at all but simply a sensory faculty not yet understood. Another case in point was the use of electrical fields by eels living in fresh water with poor visibility. These eels can sense and discriminate among other species that enter their electrical fields. According to the once accepted definition of the existing sensory systems, these eels possessed e.s.p.

The conversation soon came around to psychic communication in humans, and being thoroughly imprinted on the accepted doctrines of science by this point in their schooling, the students imitated their teachers satisfactorily. Not only were they convinced that humans do not possess e.s.p., animals were out of the question, and Steve offered a word of finality on the subject: what difference would it make? All we can do is rely on the empirically measurable. End of discussion.

Well, not quite. Candy harbored some doubts, and though somewhat fearful of rejection by the other students, asked me what I thought about e.s.p. I recounted a few experiences in my life which had convinced me that it exists. I mentioned the time during class break at the University of Washington when I commented to a couple of students that Elvis Presley would die soon. Why those words ever came from my mouth, I hadn't the foggiest notion, but one of the students entered my comment in her personal diary that evening. That same evening Elvis did die, and it was not until the student brought me the passage in her diary that I recalled having said what I did. That was only the beginning, however, and I went on to describe a similar incident several months later when I was driving with a friend from Bellingham to Seattle and suddenly expressed an intuition that "a great singer will die today." My friend queried me for more information but I had none. Several hours later in the day a gas station attendant who was washing our window said that a news broadcast had just announced the death of Bing Crosby in Spain.

Crosby's death had not been announced until after my intuition about "a great singer," but at the time I had it he may have already been dead. Perhaps I was receiving radio or TV broadcasts being transmitted from Spain hours before the news broke on the west coast. As for Elvis, my prediction was made at least twelve hours before his death.

The students resisted the plausibility of my personal experiences; they feared believing something which could harm their professional careers. I went on to say that only twice in my life had I predicted deaths, the first time I accurately named the person, the second time I didn't name the person; though many singers would not fall within the description of "great," Bing Crosby certainly did.

Because I had experienced a psychic communication with orcas, and I wanted to be able to open the students' minds to the possible, I proposed that we conduct a small experiment then and there on psychic communication. We all sat down next to Skana at the end of the large pool, and Skana stayed there with us, opening her mouth and protruding her tongue, inviting us to scratch it, something orcas are fond of. I told everyone to avoid physical contact with Skana for the time being, and asked each student to stand up, walk to their right around the pool to the platform on the far side and then sit down in a quasi-lotus posture with their eyes closed on the edge of the pool. I told them to sit there silently while we counted to a hundred, to avoid making any movements or sounds, then, when the next person in line replaced them, to stand up and walk around the rest of the pool back to the group and sit down.

The first two students followed the instructions properly, and throughout these trials Skana stayed at the end of the pool with the rest of us. I went third and behaved exactly as they had with one difference: as soon as I sat down with my eyes closed I did not count, but I did concentrate on Skana and said these words silently in my mind. "Skana, if you hear me then come to me. Come to me Skana and show me that you read my thoughts." The students were observing me and taking notes on Skana's behavior. Within five seconds after I sat down I heard the sound of Skana emerging immediately in front of me, and when I opened my eyes there she was with her head pointed straight at mine a few inches away. I closed my eyes and continued mentally concentrating on Skana and silently repeated these words,"Thank you Skana for hearing me, thank you for showing me."

When I stood up and returned to the group, Skana swam back to the end of the pool where we were. The students were awed by what they had seen, and wanted to know what I had done, but I told them that we had to complete the experiment, so the last two followed the routine with expected results: Skana stayed with the group.

When the last student returned I explained to them what I had done differently than them, and we concluded that perhaps psychic communication with other beings is possible after all. I reminded them that our evidence was not conclusive, that in principle many experiments would need to be conducted, and that in light of serious research in e.s.p., it might be expected that not everyone nor every orca would produce the same results. Intentions are vitally important in all forms of communication, and a person who repeated my covert behavior without really believing in his psychic ability or that of the orca may fail.

In the same way that Toni's attitudes towards White Wing governed White Wing's behavior toward her, a skeptic about e.s.p. might influence results negatively. That is precisely what e.s.p. research has found: many people guessing cards performed way below the level of chance, so poorly in fact that the only statistical explanation was that they had to have known what the right answers were to make so many wrong ones. Perhaps right thinking would create right living. Perhaps right minds make right worlds.

A 'Talking' Whale

W E MADE MANY VISITS to the Vancouver Aquarium to conduct behavioral studies on orcas, and to prepare students for identification and description of behavior of wild orcas. It's always a good idea for students to compare and contrast different species so I encouraged them to spend some time observing the aquarium's belugas, small angelic whales closely related to the orca and other delphinids.

When the students told me that they thought the male beluga was phonating his name, I came to the aquarium with recording equipment, and sure enough, he was saying "Logosi." This was the first instance recorded of any cetacean clearly imitating human language in "real time," at a frequency immediately discernible to the human listener without having to slow down tape recordings, as in dolphin research. The discovery is immensely significant because it suggests that it might be possible to teach vocal language directly to belugas, which has proved impossible with other toothed whales.

Captive since infancy, Logosi was about fifteen years old, and may have lived longer in captivity at that time than any whale. He was contained with two females in a small, elliptical pool used for periodic tourist shows involving all the belugas. The pool was the usual sterile environment, effectively just a large bath tub, lacking stimulation except from trainers and tourists. Logosi was especially attracted to humans at the underwater viewing windows, and he spent as much or more time at them interacting with people than with the female belugas, which avoided the windows, possibly because Logosi claimed them aggressively.

Much of the time Logosi swam in large circles around the tank stopping at a window with a person outside. His preference for interaction with people at the windows was usually interrupted only by the tourist shows in which he performed.

When we told the aquarium personnel that Logosi could say his name, one trainer was already aware of this and mentioned during the beluga show that Logosi "'knows how to say his name." The trainers frequently say "Logosi" over a loudhaler during the shows which entail reinforcement of all belugas with frozen herring, their staple diet. Logosi had heard his name above and probably below water countless times in close association with being fed, but no one had deliberately taught him his own name.

Though food reinforcement might conceivably explain the unintentional conditioning of Logosi's imitation of his name, it could not account for all his predictable behavior interacting with us and other humans at the windows. Initially, Logosi faced and made eye to eye contact before pressing his melon, the bulbous forehead containing sinuses which figure in sound production normally transmitted from the apex of the jaw bones, against the window and transmitting sound through it to the human. With the melon against the glass communicating sound, he'd gape, opening and closing his mouth as though imitating the jaw movements of talking humans. It's important to stress that belugas do not emit sounds from their throat. They have no vocal cord, but rely exclusively on the complex system of sinuses in the melon which contract and pass air through passages between them to make sound.

After a period of eye contact, transmitting sound through the window and gaping, Logosi turned his head sideways placing it against or close to the glass as though he were listening to the vocal response of humans. As some people did turn their ears to the window while Logosi phonated, he may have been imitating the behavior of listening humans. While apparently listening for human voice, Logosi did not produce sounds or gape. Whether or not humans vocalized, Logosi resumed phonating from the frontal position for awhile before returning to the listening stance, and so on for up to several minutes at a window.

The sounds transmitted through the glass resembled garbled human voices as heard underwater, perhaps an imitation of what Logosi heard from humans through the glass and water medium. Only "Logosi" was clearly perceptible. To test our perhaps too hopeful impressions, we played tape recordings of Logosi's sounds to naive listeners who said they could hear the word "Logosi" and described the rest as garbled voices (human) or Russian. The calls of free ranging belugas have been likened to the sound of children playing in the distance.

Belugas have quite large brains. Using John Lilly's logarithmic scale of brain to body weight, the beluga's brain ranks as large or larger than that of the human, orca and sperm whale. And belugas are extremely vocal, possibly the most vocal cetacean. Early on in the whaling era they earned the nickname "canary of the sea." They are adapted to feed in the murky waters of coastlines and rivers, where vocal communication could be important in locating food and cooperating to avoid predators including the orca and man. All of which suggests that the beluga is as fine a candidate for interspecies communication research as exists among whales and dolphins.

In playback experiments, D. Morgan documented that in wild belugas both syntax and context are important, and that certain specific sounds and certain combinations have specific meanings. In short, his results further corroborate our assessment that belugas are ideal subjects for exploring the possibility of linguistic communication with another species.

Before the scientific report on Logosi appeared, an animal newsletter got wind of our discovery of the "talking whale." The editor hounded me for more information, and reluctantly, I gave him some facts of the case and why, we felt, belugas could make ideal subjects for research in interspecies communication.

Hungry for more information and a big scoop, the editor contacted the Vancouver Aquarium, and was put in touch with the curator, who raved in the ensuing story that Logosi couldn't 'talk,' that, like a parrot, he was only imitating human voice. We hadn't said anything different. Since then, a Purdue scientist has discovered that parrots may just be doing more than parroting, but in any case, the curator discredited us for making claims that Logosi could talk—which was the editor's doing, not ours—while making all kinds of broad generalizations about how no beluga or dolphin has human intelligence or the capacity for language. As if he knew.

The sadly comic aspect of the story was that the curator went ahead to say, contrary to our impression, that Logosi's sounds resembled Chinese more than Russian. Logosi was captured in arctic waters frequented by Russian ships, and anyone who has listened underwater with a hydrophone to radio broadcasts amplified by shiphulls, may appreciate that a beluga whale might conceivably become imprinted to the sound of Russian.

As fate had it, the editor's inquiries and subsequent story prompted the curator, who hadn't noticed us until then, to oust us from the aquarium. Our research could no longer be conducted there because the nonsense about 'talking whales' caste a poor, meaning unscientific, image on the curator and the facility. But they couldn't prevent us from coming as paying customers.

Nonetheless, our plan to set up a slide screen outside Logosi's tank, which he could view through the submerged window, and present slides of objects while broadcasting their English names to see if he would begin to develop a vocabulary and eventually ask for certain pictures or combine words to describe new images, a step towards use of language, was thwarted. Entirely at our expense and effort, with no bother to the aquarium or its business short of permission to hang a hydrophone in Logosi's pool and set up a screen outside it, not only might we have been able to make some serious progress exploring his linguistic capacity, we would have generated much interest in the aquarium.

To this day, only musician Jim Nollmon has seized the opportunity to employ these highly vocal, large, brained cetaceans for interspecies communication work. Oddly enough, the Vancouver Aquarium had since incorporated Logosi's "talking" into its publicity program. But Logosi died.

Discouraged by a series of setback resulting from human resistance to our objectives to decipher orca communication, we relocated to Ashland, Oregon. It was inevitable, I suppose, that not much later the *National Enquirer* would appear. After losing an inherited fortune trying to keep the whale work alive, and surviving by our bootstraps, we weighed the risks of the *National Enquirer* effectively discrediting legitimate research findings against the possible advantages of reaching millions of people and our use of the $2,500 royalty offered for an interview and a couple of photos of Logosi.

The reporter asked me questions while he tape-recorded our conversation, and I did my utmost to make statements that were accurate and precise, beyond distortion or readily taken out of context. He kept digging for one thing, for me to say that Logosi was a talking whale. And the more he tried dredging this out of me the more anxious I became. I stopped the interview to ask him to agree in writing that I would have the right to veto anything in his story. His song and dance routine was well rehearsed, and he kept assuring me that he'd quote only what was on the tape, nothing more, and offered me a legal contract to that effect.

He took us out to dinner after the interview, and what transpired that evening confirmed my doubts. The guy had a few too many drinks, thank God, and as the night wore he shared with us stories about his reporting adventures for the *Enquirer,* to which we were most attentive.

The *Enquirer* had assigned him to write a story about a shrine in India where, twice daily, when the priests came to pray, the cobras also appeared and prayed, a reference to the snakes holding their heads up high to face the altar. Quite a story. At the shrine, our man found no cobras during prayer hour, so to complete his assignment he hired a couple of locals to search for snakes, but they found only one, insufficient to serve his purpose of constructing a photo with priests and several snakes together at prayer. He could concoct the story easily enough, but not without a credible photo. Next he set out to employ the service of snake charmers who would line up their cobras against a backdrop of praying priests.

On the way back to the temple with four snake charmers holding cobras in baskets on their laps, the Indian driving the taxi ignored our man's warnings to slow down, and hit a deep rut which threw everyone in the car including the four cobras against the roof. With four cobras loose in the car, the reporter thought to throw his camera bag out the window before he opened the door and jumped for his life as the car careened off the road into a pond. The last he saw of them, the driver, charmers and snakes were swimming for shore.

His mission failed, but that was just one of several stories about how the *Enquirer* manages to convert fiction into fact for its readers. Next morning I wired the officers of the *Enquirer* demanding that nothing I said be used by them.

The day may come when we can talk about "talking" animals without threat of censure, condemnation or distortion. On the one extreme are whale enthusiasts who have seen the Hollywood movie, "Day of the Dolphin," with its "talking" dolphins, and read some of John Lilly's work, on which the fictional movie plot is based. Perhaps they grew up on TV's

"Flipper," but altogether they have failed to separate fact from fiction and when someone tells them that dolphin language has not been deciphered or that Lilly isn't conducting conversations with dolphins, that he never did and certainly never said so, they are shocked. On the other extreme are the super-humanists who, without considering the information and theories behind the scientific efforts to establish interspecies communication with cetaceans proclaim that only humans have language and that no other species possibly could have the intelligence to ever acquire or use language.

P.S. The college president where I taught was a Jesuit. He heard from my students that animals are intelligent, and that some may have language or more advanced communication. Jack asked the students to ask me if any animals had written a symphony lately. My answer was that if ability to compose a symphony is what separates humans from animals then very few people qualify.

6

Making Friends with Wild Orcas

"**D**ID YOU SEE THAT! She swam right up to me. The calf too. Only three feet away. They looked right at me. Wow! That was worth the whole trip. I'll never forget that as long as I live!"

So went the exclamation of Old College student Vicki Case as she emerged from the 45-degree water of Johnstone Strait, British Columbia. She had just experienced an encounter of the third kind. She had come face to face, eye to eye with an intelligent extraterrestrial being.

Vicki Case and Malcolm Myles were among the lucky few who will one day say to their grandkids that they looked wild orcas straight in the eye. And when they did they saw something special, an intelligent, aware creature looking at them. This ruler of the seas seems able to communicate its advanced awareness to anyone fortunate enough to see them close up.

As Loren Eiseley said in *The Unexpected Universe*, for the soul to come home to itself, after its long and terrible journey, a man must see his reflection in an eye other than human. And even Aristotle acknowledged that dolphins were intelligent and in possession of a language, albeit other than Greek judging by their accent!

Paying homage to the whales was not all we did in going north to Cracroft Island and camping without all conveniences miles from civilization. No, our expeditions meant still more: we discovered the meaning of authentic education. As Gary Snyder put it when he came to lecture, we have education turned around. Rather than read the animal's tracks (books), we should observe the animal that makes them. Then the tracks have meaning. That we did indeed: direct experience of the world is what gives genuine meaning to ideas, theories and book learning.

Though one could never adequately describe experience—Krishnamurti reminds us often that "the word is not the thing"—what happened on that island was positively life changing. The most marvelous transformations occurred spontaneously there as we found ourselves living close to the earth, dependent upon one another and upon the earth without all the man-made barriers of techno-civilization. We discovered how well equipped we are by nature to cooperate, to observe, listen, feel, and contemplate. We found the meaning of silence, the precious value of simplicity, clear, clean air, and doing things for ourselves and one another harmoniously. What revealed itself was community, not only human but the whole community of which we are a part. In another word, we uncovered the most basic sense of religion—reuniting.

At 6:30 Susan was out in the Easy Rider kayak hoping to find orcas on Johnstone Strait. For the previous three days no orcas had come by our camp—longest period without orcas in three summers. In 1984 Susan also had served as a volunteer in the Orca Project, and on her last day went out into the Strait in a kayak. The photo she took of a large bull orca surfacing right next to her is the best orca photo any of us have seen. Her greatest desire on her last day this year was to be close again to the orcas.

At 6:45 Susan began yelling, "Orcas! Orcas East! Orcas!" I

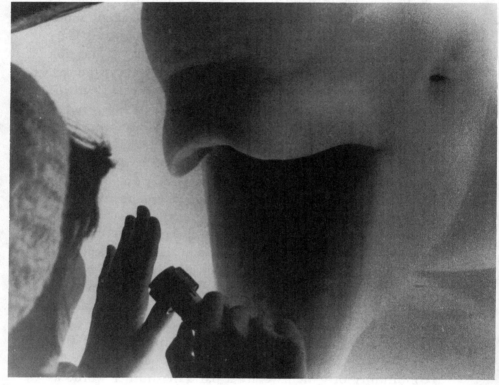

TONI L. RACE

Logosi was the first cetacean to imitate human speech in real time.

TONI L. RACE

Logosi the "talking whale" imitating the gestures of human speech while transmitting sounds including his name through the glass at the Vancouver Aquarium.

ran to the observation post and saw them hanging at the surface a half-mile east, just off shore and facing in Susan's direction at mid-channel. Orcas spend very little time motionless on the surface but the bull, cow and calf were "hanging" for a long period. I knew they were ready to interact with us so I yelled to the camp, "Orcas. They're ready. Come on, get up. This is what we came for. Let's go!"

Leigh Ann and Deanna stumbled from their tents onto the beach and I explained that the orcas were in a receptive mood, that we'd be able to get close to them, and to hurry up.

By the time we were on the water, the orcas had been around Susan and the kayak for several minutes. While waiting in the boat, I snapped shots of them spy-hopping her—rising up out of the water head-first to use their eyes above water and look at her. A male swam on his side along her boat and slapped his pectoral fin down after holding it up and waving at her as though gesturing hello. There is no other interpretation possible—orcas wave their pectoral fins only at humans. The calf was breaching and tail-lobbing.

When we pulled up and cut the engine about 100 feet from Susan the orcas had dived and she was scanning the water waiting for them to surface. She said that it was Abe, known in scientific annals as A-5, and Nicola. Further across the strait we saw other orcas, Asix (A-6), Cola (resembling Nicola but without the nick in her dorsal fin) and another cow.

Over the next two hours we moved ahead of the orcas, killed the engine and waited for them to come by the boat so we could photograph and film them in the ideal light on smooth water when they were in a relaxed mood and playful. It was the first real opportunity in eleven days to get to know Nicola's pod better.

At the intersection of West Cracroft and Blackfish Sound the orcas were apparently feeding, but when we stopped the boat 100 yards away they surfaced together and hung on the surface. The calf leaped back and forth over Nicola's back; twice it twisted 180 degrees in the air and landed on its backside. Repeatedly it slapped its fluke against the water, and did a front breach directly toward us. Then I called out, "Nicola!" Nicola swam closer to us, about thirty yards off and stopped and hung on the surface. The calf followed her and so did Cola. It hadn't occurred to me until after spontaneously calling her name that she might know our name for her. Jeff Jacobsen and others working with the orcas surely had spoken her name hundreds of times in close proximity to her. Perhaps I had found a direct, obvious way to communicate and establish closer ties to Nicola and her group.

A mile or so into Blackfish Sound we laughed over and over at the antics of the calf—more breaching, still fluke-slapping each time we passed on his right or he swam past the boat. Then we saw a Minke whale, common prey of transient orcas in some areas, swim directly into the pod of orcas. The orcas were moving north as a phalanx, clustered within a radius of perhaps 20 yards, and the Minke was headed south. When the orcas were about 100 feet from the Minke, they dived in unison exactly when the Minke dived. There was no attack. Though we didn't see the Minke surface again, the orcas came right up where it had dived, within 20 seconds, not enough time to kill or feed on a Minke whale—and there was no blood slick either. The calf seemed overly excited after passing the Minke underwater.

Small groups of Dall's porpoises surfaced and blew and dived frequently as the orcas swam around and past them. Orcas have also killed and eaten Dall's porpoises, but not here, at least not the residents. Only transient orcas have been observed attacking porpoises and other marine mammals.

Later in the same month, Nicola made another special appearance, this time at dark. She had come alone around the observation point, and everyone who had called her name out from the post above the water began to run across the beach to intercept her as she passed close by the opposite shore. We stopped at the beach when we noticed that Nicola had stopped in the cove. She was hanging on the surface about 50 feet away with her head pointed towards us.

After three minutes, Nicola slowly reoriented herself to the rocks at the north side of the cove. She moved a few feet closer to the rocks, and remained on the surface, blowing occasionally. Dorene Pratt was squatting there below her tent, and talking softly to Nicola. Dorene had worked closely with Hardy Jones, and helped him produce the fascinating film of dolphins interacting with divers underwater. I eased around behind Dorene to observe their interaction. For twenty minutes, Nicola stayed only five feet away from Dorene, apparently listening to her small talk. It was the longest connection I ever witnessed between a solitary, wild orca and a human. Dorene felt as though she had definitely communicated with Nicola, and their interaction further inspired our efforts to establish friendly relationships with wild orcas.

I was eating dinner around the campfire on the beach with the next group of volunteers when Nicola swam across the cove. She was moving slowly on the surface, rather than diving and surfacing. As one man, ten volunteers set down their plates and ran to the observation post, where Nicola was headed.

When as a group we called with pure enthusiasm to her, Nicola stopped, oriented to us on shore and apparently called her clan together. Her female kin and their younger calves assembled in one large group immediately in front of the observation post where we stood. They "hung" on the surface facing us as we yelled, "Nicola! Nicola! Nicola! Hey Nicola, come here Nicola! Ooowee." We laughed and giggled and jumped up and down as all the orcas watched us watching them.

Two at a time, the orca cows swam directly to us with a calf as the other orcas remained assembled on the surface. The single calf in each envoy spyhopped over and over, it's head coming straight up out of the water to look at us on the post. None of the cows spyhopped, but the delegations continued until all the calves had spied us close up.

I believe that Nicola and her adult female kin introduced

their babies to a pod of friendly, excited humans—a true communion between species and the high point of twenty years of field work. As I ended a poem to Nicola, "the real work of whale watching is the meeting of nations."

After the cows and calves in their small subgroups had come in to see us and left, everyone realized for the first time that they hadn't brought their cameras to the most spectacular event in orcaland. No cameras, a lesson there. Nothing between hearts. Magic happens when we're children enough to let it. So far the best technique for attracting, befriending and communicating with wild orcas has been simply calling them. A state of innocence may promote the meeting of nations.

During the last group's visit, there was nothing spectacular between the orcas and us. After hearing of the summer's events with orcas, but having experienced the ordinary all week the volunteers were discouraged. Their last day I organized an excursion on a fishing boat to Alert Bay and the cannery. Only Christy Barker had stayed in camp hoping that she might be there if the orcas made a stop to see us.

At 6:00 PM I went up to the post with Lou Ann, and soon Nicola and her pod appeared in front heading west. Just as Christy walked up to the post I said to her and Lou Ann, "O.K., let's call to her in unison as loud as we can. Ready, now, on three. One, two, three." And we yelled, "Nicola! Nicola! Nicola!" Nicola performed a full body breach right in front of us, and during the breach she turned ninety degrees to the side and faced us, apparently to look directly at us with both eyes while she was airborne.

Christy had been skeptical, I think, of my description of what had transpired during the summer, but she became a believer, and not only did she return for her third year as a volunteer, she set sail for an advanced degree in marine mammalogy. So ended the most rewarding summer of human-orca connections, and I was even more enthused about what to expect the following year.

We did a lot of calling the third summer, but to little avail.

Though we kept it up for weeks, I sensed early on that it wouldn't work. Orcas and dolphins are notorious in captivity for becoming easily bored. The game or trick for today is apt to be gone tomorrow. Nicola did indicate her recognition of me, I think, when Efale and I called to her from the boat in the middle of the Strait. Nicola and her closest associates, another cow and calf, simultaneously stood on their heads side by side with their tails above water waving directly at us. Except in aquariums, that was the only time I've seen orcas wave their flukes at people. (See Meta-communication between dolphins and humans for similar account of wild orcas.)

Rachel Henderson and her family interacted for several hours one night with orcas by the post. It was the only case in three years of orcas staying in one place for more than twenty minutes—Dorene Pratt's "conversation" with Nicola. Even when they're resting, orcas continue moving ahead and diving periodically, but these orcas stayed on the surface and vocalized as Rachel imitated their sounds and sang to them. Judging from their time of arrival, they may have been the same orcas who visited Jim Nollman's camp down at Boat Bay earlier that night. Jim interacts with orcas via music, and has produced a phenomenal tape of acoustic exchanges between himself and orcas. His recordings made that evening sounded like Nicola's pod, so perhaps it was Nicola and her group who later visited our camp and interacted acoustically with Rachel.

It was an eventful summer in other ways: several times we had directly observed orcas catching salmon; the orcas often passed our shores within a few feet; my Newfoundland, Huey, swam unharmed with the orcas as they surrounded a huge spring salmon hiding in a tidal pool; and we finally mastered salmon fishing, which meant fine dinners.

The most startling interaction came on the next to last day of the 1986 season. I took a group of volunteers out in the big red inflatable to photograph orcas in the Strait. Three pods were moving slowly in a rest pattern toward a point of convergence just off the Sophia Islands next to our camp. By the time we were launched, the orcas were beset by forty boats including private yachts, whale-watching boats, scientists, kayakers and film-makers. As we approached the encircling horde, the orcas woke up, and each group turned around and headed back as fast as they could go in the direction from which they had come. Clearly, their rest had been disturbed.

We followed Nicola's pod along Cracroft Island to Hanson Island. As I went around the orcas, passing them on the left one hundred yards out, we called out Nicola's name. The orcas behaved peculiarly. They aligned themselves in single file, parallel to the shore and to our direction of movement; as we passed one, it immediately turned around 180 degrees and swam directly back about thirty yards, then turned 180 degrees again, swam ahead for about thirty yards, and then repeated the entire thing. I was dumbfounded by these seemingly nonsensical maneuvers.

I sped the boat to get well ahead, then killed the engine and waited for them to pass alongside. When the three youngsters of the pod came by, again we called out Nicola's name. They veered sharply to the right and headed straight in to shore where they seemed to convene for a few seconds. Then they put on a great show for us: lined up side by side, they leaped out of the water in unison, exhibiting front breaches interspersed with short dives, as dolphins so often do in captivity. Moving fast, they passed immediately in front of the boat and headed toward mid-channel as an adult male followed behind them eighty yards. This was the first year that the youngsters had struck out on their own, and when they did a bull followed apparently keeping a close eye on them.

Excited by their exceptional behavior, we pursued them in the boat. At mid-channel they turned abruptly east and began porpoising, an orca's fastest "gait." At full throttle I could barely stay up with them. The youngsters still were in the side-to-side patterns, porpoising in perfect unison, and the bull continued to bring up the rear. Only once had I watched an orca employ porpoise-swimming—it was a bull pursuing a grey whale in the Strait. But the youngsters were not pursuing anything we could see, and neither did they stop anywhere to fish. For five miles they swam at top speed in a straight direction, and we followed. When they reached the mouth of Growler's cove next to the Sophia Islands and our camp, they suddenly dived and disappeared for several minutes. They surfaced a mile away along Cracroft Island heading directly back to Hanson Island where we had started the wild orca chase.

That evening I rehearsed it all in my mind. Had the orcas led us back to our camp? The same youngsters had come in with the cows to meet us last summer. They had swam with us the year before that, and hundreds of times for two summers they had seen us on the shore at camp calling out Nicola's name. And surely they knew the sound of our boat's engine. Were the young orcas trying to communicate something to us? That they know where our camp is?

Then I recalled the strange behavior along Hanson when the orcas repeatedly reversed their directions, pointing straight back towards our camp, the same direction they eventually led us. Was that an abstract signal meant to communicate, "You go that way, to your camp"?

But why would they lead us back? Just to let us know they know where we camp? The scenario may have been prompted by the disturbance of their rest by all the boats. Perhaps the orcas were simply asking us to stop disturbing them, and that is why they first changed directions, then led us home.

When I described the story to Paul Spong he didn't think my speculations were silly. He commented "Lots of times in the old days I followed the orcas in the kayak, and they would play with me, but then lead me back home as if to say, 'O.K., its been fun but enough is enough.'" I also told Spong about how the whale-watching boats had disturbed the orcas, and we agreed that real problems were brewing. Already the orcas were having to run the gauntlet of commercial fishing boats, including in the only orca reserve, Robson Bight. Some orcas were caught in fishing nets as they chased salmon along them, and for this orcas were shot and killed. Ninety percent of their primary food, salmon, were being caught by the fishermen, and I suspect that orcas are having to spend a lot more time and energy simply feeding themselves. On top of a declining food source, the breeding streams for salmon have been polluted by clearcutting, which means that fisherman and orcas will compete more seriously as the fish stocks keep declining. Add direct disturbance from whale-watching and study, and the woes of orcas couldn't be much worse.

The Johnstone Strait is unique among sites in the world for the number and density of orcas it enjoys in the summer and fall. Though whale-watching will continue, perhaps it should be eliminated altogether from Johnstone Strait except from the shore. I also would favor cessation of commercial fishing there, as ultimately the most important resource for northern British Columbia is the orca. It is where they are observed most often to rest, perhaps because its linear shape and the currents and winds are conducive. It is where interactions between groups are most observed, and if Spong is right, the Strait is where the orcas come together to "potlatch." Births and matings have been seen there.

More people will pay more money to see orcas in Johnstone Strait than the waters or the surrounding land may earn from other uses. Now we must figure out *how* to balance growing interest in orca-watching with the interests of the orcas. Of several solutions I am convinced. The scientists should quit using special privileges which allow them to pursue orcas closely; graduate students from Humboldt State and Santa Cruz have been most abusive, even ruining the orcas' feeding efforts, and by their example, encouraging tourists to do the same.

If Robson Bight is officially an Ecological Reserve for Killer Whales then it should be treated as such by the local fishermen and authorities. It is stupid for the volunteer warden, who himself operates a whale-watching business, to condemn a kayaker for passing closer than 300 yards to orcas inside the Reserve when at the same time forty boats are allowed to set nets there—nets that have caught and drowned orcas. That "they have always fished there" is a poor excuse for lack of regulation. Its a reserve or it isn't.

Because the orcas conveniently pass close by the shores of Johnstone Strait, orca-watching and study may proceed effectively without the use of boats, pursuit and disturbance. Spong stopped doing so years ago; Nollman never has. Hopefully the community of commercial whale-watchers and scientists will see fit to follow suit and encourage the ban among newcomers to the Strait.

In 1994, we conducted the Orca Project in Puget Sound. Early in the field season our volunteers included a family with a 2-year old son. The father was extremely left-brained, and he doubted that orcas could be as aware or intelligent as a human.

About half way through the expedition the father and his son rode in my boat. We came upon an orca pod on the west side of the island and followed them along the shore as they fished. The little boy sat between his father's legs at the bow of the boat. The boy saw the dorsal fin of an adult rise and sink a few feet away, and he responded by screaming. The very moment he stopped screaming a calf orca breached immediately in front of our boat. The calf orca oriented to the bow, and it was looking directly at the small boy.

The father turned around with the child in his arms and said, "Wow, did you see that? I'd swear that orca was looking right at my son."

That evening after dinner around the campfire the man sat down next to me and said, "You know you may be right after all. They may be aware."

When my slides came back I noticed that the snapshot I took of the calf orca breaching in front of us indicated that it was looking directly at the child.

I believe that orca whales perceive human sounds so accurately that they can understand the thoughts and feelings associated with the sound. To a lesser degree, we often do the same thing with music and speech.

Skana meets the author at the Vancouver Aquarium, 1979.

B.S. and A.S.

OVER THE YEARS OF CONDUCTING THE ORCA PROJECT I observed time and again that groups of volunteers created their own reality, as all of us do all the time. Higher forces seem to have been at work at bringing people together. During 1991, 94 and 95 we had one very bad group in which people pissed and moaned about this and that, and we also had a highly exceptional group each of these years.

The best group of Orca Project 94 congealed instantly. They were highly spiritual and enthusiastic. On their first morning they were ready to pray together, hand in hand around the

Hyak performing
at Vancouver
Aquarium, 1979.
RANDALL L. EATON

Miracle, first baby
orca to survive in
captivity, at Sealand
of Victoria, 1979.
RANDALL EATON

campfire. Their fervent prayers included asking for the sky to clear and finding the orcas close to Deer Harbor.

An hour later we launched our fleet of small inflatable boats under clear skies. Between Jones Island and San Juan Island we ran into a pod of orcas moving south. The orcas were closer to Deer Harbor than I had ever seen them. For three summers I operated field study expeditions out of Deer Harbor, and in the late 70s I lived there and went out in a boat every day for a year, but never did I see orcas that close to the harbor.

"A-Team" observed orcas every day during their expedition. From '91 through '95 there were 17 volunteer groups, but only one of these observed orcas every day. No other group observed orcas more than half their days on the water.

When people of like mind and pure hearts join together they hold great power. A-Team had it all together. They were present, unafraid, confident, and full of faith in themselves, the orcas and life itself. They energized their collective prayers that morning with toning—chanting together to send prayers out into the universe.

They knew what they wanted, they asked for it and they got it. We do create our own reality.

Over the years we had been in the water with orcas on many occasions. Sometimes these were deliberate as when we were camped on West Cracroft Island and could see the orcas coming our way. At other times we were scuba diving or snorkeling and the orcas came nearby. Consistently, those individuals who were sonically blasted by orcas were transformed. Many claimed that they never felt better or that their hearts had been opened. Some have claimed that it was the most important experience of their lives.

It's probably the same phenomenon as occurs in the dolphin swim centers in Florida, where dolphins use sound not only to diagnose people's injuries, diseases and energetic imbalances, but also use sound to heal them.

During the sixth expedition of '94 two people had entered the water with orcas. One of them, David McIlhenney, an attorney in Reno, felt it was a very profound experience. On the last expedition that year Charles Baltzell decided he wanted to be in the sea with orcas. Charles had been an army diver. He is the head of a holistic health organization known as the River of Life. Charles is highly sophisticated psycho-spiritually. For example, he spent ten years living in India studying with a guru whom, he says, teleports thousands of miles instantaneously, to communicate with him.

It was nearly dark when Charles got in the water the second time with the orcas. The first time he hadn't noticed much. He held onto the side of the boat as the orcas approached and swam underneath. When he came out of the water he said that they had zapped him with sound, and he felt his whole chest open up. His heart center had been expanded a lot.

When we got back to camp, Charles went straight to his tent and collapsed there with all his clothes and boots still on. He slept a deadman's sleep for 12 hours. At one point after dinner we went to check on him, wondering if he was alright. He was breathing so we left him alone.

At breakfast Charles presented a program about the profound influence that the orcas had had on him. He redefined his life in terms of B.S and A.S., that is before scan by orca and after scan by orca. He said that the sonic scan from the orcas had transformed him and that it was his most profound experience.

7

A Sorrowful
Communion with Hyak

"AFTER SEEING ORCAS IN THE WILD, I don't know if I could stand seeming them all cooped up, but I suppose I should see one up close. I never have," Susan said as we drove through North Vancouver. "Yeah. Yeah, you really should. So, you want to look an orca in the eye, huh?," I responded. "Well, I feel like I should." "No time like the present. The aquarium's just on our way, in Stanley Park. And you're absolutely right. Everyone who comes up on the project should stop by here and look an orca in the eye. That's important."

In the late 70s I had made several trips to the Vancouver Aquarium to help students who were doing interns with our whale study group. Skana and Hyak were the orcas at that time; Skana was an adult female, Hyak a young adult male. Skana died, and Hyak now lives with two young orcas from Iceland.

My visits to the aquarium had been quite eventful: discovering Logosi the white whale who was imitating human speech; experiencing telepathic communication with Skana; and, encountering orca, dolphin and beluga personalities up close—

and their severe boredom. These few visits meant only passing interaction with Hyak. My time was spent with Skana or Logosi and the students. In fact I never actually touched Hyak, and spent perhaps an hour sitting by his pool with him one morning. Even then our interaction was not memorable.

On the way to the parking lot in Stanley Park I wondered if I could justify the time, with a tight schedule that included buying gear and supplies on my way home to San Juan Island. The next day was my birthday, and I much needed to rest, and the day after and all the way through the holiday period stores would be closed. On the other hand, I knew in my heart that it would be a wonderful thing for Susan to see orcas up close and experience them personally.

As we got out of the truck I started to tell her to go ahead by herself. I was too drained by the trip to withstand seeing the orcas in captivity, even though I knew Hyak a little and wanted to see the surviving beluga, too. But I grabbed my camera case and trudged up the hill, with growing eagerness on the one hand, anxiety on the other.

First we went to the underwater viewing windows around the beluga pool, smaller than the average swimming pool in Orange County. The aquarium was packed with bustling people, and the pool was surrounded by a hundred and fifty people straining to get closer. The beluga show was about to start, so we went below where we could observe; the windows were unoccupied. I went around to the same window where I met Logosi and heard him say, "Logosi," right through the glass, clear as can be.

After recounting the story to Susan, we headed to the underwater viewing area for the orcas. As we approached an open window I saw Hyak dangling from the surface. The pool wasn't deep enough to contain the full-length of his body, so his tail and fluke were curled to one side above the floor.

When we were about ten feet from the window, Susan held back as I went ahead and placed my chest, forehead and palms against the glass. In my mind I thought, "Hyak, poor Hyak.

Skana's dead. Your old friend is dead." Hyak swam straight to the window, one of a dozen or more, and pushed his forehead against the glass, flattening it out so it covered my upper chest and head. I was overcome by emotion. Skana had been my friend, too, and a great teacher to many scientists and visitors. Her tragic death, years after others had urged her release back into northern B.C. and her original pod, which was well known to us, had already brought me to tears. So I was sad to see Hyak, who seemed so terribly bored and lonely. Somehow he conveyed his suffering to me, somehow I shared my empathy and sorrow for him.

After we were together there for several minutes, my eyes closed with tears running down my face, people began to notice Hyak's interest in me and our peculiar interaction. Faintly, I overheard a boy say, "Look, he wants to kiss you." And several people laughed as others remained silent, in awe of the fact that Hyak may as well have been kissing me.

I opened my eyes and looked directly in the boy's eyes and said, "Yes he does. Yes, he wants to kiss me." Over my shoulder I glimpsed Susan, crying, standing there behind me with her clenched fists held up to her mouth. Someone else walking by said, "Boy, he's a big one. He could eat you in a second." And one older man leaned over and asked softly, "What is he doing. Does he know you?" I answered only, "Yes."

Ten minutes went by before Hyak went up for air, then returned to the glass and resumed the same posture with his head pushed against me. In my mind I kept telling him how sorry I was, that I knew it wasn't easy for him, as I experienced waves of his pain flowing through me. It was as if he were my brother, and his only friend and companion in the world, who had as much as raised him, had died. Throughout our interaction, I was sending love from my heart center, and loving thoughts from my third eye and hands, and there was one time when I envisioned my open arms around his body, moving from his head down to his tail. At the same time, his body shuddered with a visible ripple from head to tail which precisely accompanied my imaginary caresses. We were in perfect communion.

To my knowledge no other orca in captivity has behaved these ways with a human, and it was the only time I saw Hyak press his head against the glass. We spent nearly 40 minutes together, Hyak leaving twice to breath, and when it was time for his show to begin, he went to the place in the pool where he always waited for the opening command. I admired his stalwart devotion as he put on another great performance, apparently bored with himself yet steadfast in exciting another crowd. I believe he held no malice towards humans, nor any blame for the loss of his dear partner, and I believe he accepts his destiny as a conveyor of good will between his people and ours.

Susan watched the entire communion that day, and when the show started we comforted one another silently. More tears for Hyak and ourselves. After the show, we went up to the seating area around the pool and interacted visually with Hyak, who turned his head sideways and watched us through one eye for an hour. The young orcas soon followed suit, so that all three were visually focusing on us wherever we moved. They ignored other humans, some of whom noticed our connection with them. Finally the arrogant trainer could restrain himself no longer and said, "They know you, don't they? They must know you." We shook our heads yes, and left.

During the following year I often dreamed of Hyak, and more. I came to feel that I was in constant communication with him, and that, somehow, he had connected me on a spiritual plane with his entire nation. Each day I pause to send him my love—and thanks. For me, Hyak is a living spirit guardian. Thousands of people look at Hyak, and enjoy him, but they never *see* or feel him. That is the greatest tragedy of all. To many he's just a big fish with the reputation of a killer.

8

The Orca Is
'One Step Above God'

MAN IS THE TOOL USING ANIMAL. Man is altruistic. Man makes art. Man uses language. Only man is aware of death. Man thinks. Each vision of ourselves as special and unique has crumbled: other animals use tools, many species are highly altruistic. Chimpanzees paint pictures and use sign-language, certainly numerous creatures think and reason, and though we cannot say with absolute certainty that other life-forms are not aware of death, the behavior of elephants with dying and dead companions and the manner in which they seen to muse over the bones of comrades suggests some understanding of death, and the same may be said of dying cetaceans who purposefully strand themselves on land, accompanied in some cases by their group members who give the impression of conducting mournful burial rites.

What is biologically unique about humanity recently and presently is none of the usual accolades put forth by heady anthropologists, historians and philosophers, but rather its dominion over other creatures. Except for small pockets of the globe, the human has achieved full dominance over all other life forms. We are the ecological dominant, like an oak tree in a hardwood forest that outcompetes other trees for light and land, and we are the behavioral dominant, able to supplant any animal that dares contest us for right of access to resources or space. And while intelligence, language and cooperative behavior figure into our most unexpected rise to world rule, they are necessary but insufficient conditions, which, with a special category of material and the know how to use it, tells the story. Man rules his world with the weapon. He is the master of weapons, and from all appearances strives for the power of the Hindu god Shiva, destroyer of worlds.

If we are to fathom the origin of our social-ecological crisis, we must grapple with our phylogenetic heritage: how did we get here, why are we the way we are? To turn it around, now that we rule this planet, why are we experiencing such a hard time? Since our history led us to dominance, and succeeding as a dominant is our central problem, we need models to inform us, and they are few.

The orca is to the ocean what man is to the land. Like man, orca rules its domain, or did until recently challenged by man. Man and the orca are the two most formidable, successful and intelligent social predators to ever live on earth. They and the lion, which was the dominant terrestrial predator throughout most of the New and Old Worlds until a few thousand years ago, before man outcompeted it, are surprisingly alike: high ranking, cosmopolitan (the lion was the most widespread terrestrial mammal before man), highly social, polygamous predators. When we add the wolf as the dominant species of the Holarctic region, again, until usurped by man, over the past 10,000 years the list of living species that have occupied our present position is exhausted. They will be our teachers.

Next to the sperm whale, the orca's brain is largest on earth, and more highly evolved than man's. Unlike the sperm whale, the orca is extremely social and cooperates to hunt, and among higher mammals including man, may have the most stable society. Field research indicates that membership in orca groups is more constant than any species. This monarch of the dolphins may be unsurpassed in longevity—one male who spent 115 years leading Australian whalers to migrating whales which his group attacked and held at bay while the whalers harpooned them was at least 145 years old when he died an accidental death. The age of sexual maturity of the orca is fifteen years or older, in excess of the human's, and if the standard ideas about the age of sexual maturity apply, then the orca has a longer period of dependent learning than any creature known. The orca likewise excels in memory, learning and perceptual faculties.

While the human and orca converge in many ways, the orca stands alone among living ex-dominants and humans in matters of warfare, of which there are two kinds. Wolves patrol the borders of the pack's territory and if strangers intrude they are viciously attacked and killed. Male lions go in groups to make war against other males and gain rights to a territory and the females living there. Humans make war against other humans, originally perhaps for the same reason as lions, to steal wives, and they certainly war over territory and food resources. Dominant and very high-ranking species are much more likely to war against their own species because, by virtue of being highranking, it is their own kind who are most competitive for resources ranging from food to mates.

It is a biological puzzle that orcas do not make war. Competition among males for females has never been observed, and distinct social groups feed peacefully together at local sites with clumped prey resources. Some orca groups seem territorial, but intruding groups are never attacked; friendship is the rule. Despite common arguments such as, "The sea has so much food that they don't need to compete," there is no reason to expect large social predators that are primarily adapted to prey upon larger whales to be anything but competitive. Even if communication by sonar explains why war is absent, only genetic relatedness explains friendliness among resident groups which convene into "super pods."

If a feeding area can tolerate another group of twenty or thirty, then as far as the resident orcas should be concerned, they would be better off to reproduce and add their sons and daughters to their groups. There is no such thing as unlimited resources in any environment including the sea, and as for orcas, owing to human intervention, their primary food species have been radically reduced. All the more reason to suspect that some form of competition between groups would be found, at least in the better remaining waters.

To make matters more perplexing, we now turn to a second brand of war, that between different species. Not predation, the killing of other animals for food, but interspecies aggression as occurs commonly between lions and spotted hyenas, hyenas and African wild dogs, leopards and hyenas, wolves and grizzly bears, and so on. Among guild members—species that occupy similar niches in a community—direct or interference competition is commonplace. Though one lion may easily dominate several hyenas in a contest for a large animal carcass killed by one of the species, enough hyenas may not only drive the lion off and steal the food they may also kill it. These species are indirect competitors for food, that is they feed on the same populations of game animals, they prey upon one another's young as opportunities occur, and they compete quite directly for animal bodies. As a consequence, hate between species has evolved. And for good reason—from a lion's point of view, the only good hyena is a dead one, which is why, if a lion sees a hyena, he is likely to attack and kill it—but not eat it. In the absence of young lions, and with no food present or prospective food on the hoof nearby, a lion will expend its energy and time solely to kill hyenas. And examination of the lion's expressive behavior dictates clearly that the lion's mood is one of aggression, the same as displayed in fighting another lion over mating rights. This is in contrast to the neutral expression of the lion killing a zebra. The advantage of killing hyenas just because they're there is long-term: next week they night kill a lion's kittens or come with comrades to steal food.

Basically the same situation exists between the wolf and grizzly bear. One of the main reasons the wolf is social is the advantage individuals have in groups; together four or five adult wolves can best a grizzly, drive it away from a densite, protect a moose carcass or steal food from the grizzly if need be. On the other hand, grizzly bears often get several large meals by driving wolves off their kill. The outcome is a matter of numbers and ferocity, a starving grizzly in the early spring may not be worth combating unless the wolfpack is fairly large.

As for the human, no doubt it fought its way up the ladder of large predators in the same way. No matter how successful our ancestors may have been as predators of big game, and let there be no mistake that carnivory was the single most important dimension to human origins, it does no good to kill a large animal if you can't defend it. When Richard Leaky says that a man could walk around the savannas scavenging lots of meat, he overlooks the fact that lions that now run away from humans did not fear humans until fairly recently with the introduction of high powered weapons and the mass slaughter of lions in what are now national parks. Not only would it have been hard a hundred years ago to convince lions to give up a zebra, he would have faced a high risk of being attacked himself. Only in groups of highly cooperative adult males finely skilled in the use of primitive weapons could humans and their forebearers have defended big game kills against the likes of lions and hyenas.

The Masai are impressive warriors, among the most awesome warriors this planet has known in the past several thousand years. They are tall, swift, strong, and forceful. Western armies with automatic firearms were unable to defeat the shield and spear-bearing Masai who annihilated several sizable armies. Until the twentieth century, the Masai were the dominant humans in their world, but their adversary of worth was the lion. It took about a dozen Masai warriors in cooperative maneuvers and using razor-sharp steel spears and body-covering shields to kill a single male lion. Even then there were risks. One cannot fathom how humans fared against the attack of four or five adult male lions, much less how they ever could have driven twelve adults off a kill—if they did.

My point is that we were for hundreds of thousands of years right in the thick of it with other large predators, all of which were our enemies and competitors. There is good reason to believe that our oldest and longest war was not with other humans but with the lions, hyenas, wolves and bears—all of which coexisted with European humans twenty thousand years ago. Only when we fully dominated our predator enemies did other groups of humans become our major competitors, and we are still not recovered from that turn of events since it led us directly to our present crisis.

High-ranking predators make war on one another, but when we arrive at the ocean, its ruling predator lets us pass unscathed. Now we are peeking at the most remarkable fact of all: assuming that there is some way of accounting for lack of war between orcas, how can we possibly explain the fact that orcas don't kill humans?

Remember that this is not any ordinary predator, but the predator par excellence of a marine world with no shortage of predatory lifeforms. The orca has left no records unset, having killed everything from giant octopus and swift salmon to the largest creature that has lived on this planet—the blue whale. Groups of orcas have been observed to systematically encircle and eradicate entire herds of sea lions, break antarctic ice to catch resting seals, leap onto beach cliffs to grab sleeping victims, and intercept ducks in flight above the water. With an unbelievable ability to synchronize their behavior, uncanny speed underwater, clocked by a Boeing scientist at 32 knots, immense size ranging from 25 to 35 feet and several tons, and fifty conical teeth able to snap a sea lion in two with a single bite, we are not describing anything less than the most impressive predator in the history of the world before man with his firearms. No wonder the Navy would like to enlist an orca corps; with their full cooperation, every port in the world could be shut down, every enemy ship and submarine dispatched.

A predator that goes through life snapping up seals, dolphins, brant, salmon, squid, and a careless dog now and then shouldn't be adverse to grabbing a human swimmer or diver, should it? In two recorded instances when one broke ice and both a man and his dog fell through, only the dog was eaten. People have said, "Maybe they don't like the taste of humans." Possibly, but if that were the case then why haven't we any evidence that they ever sampled humans to discover how foul they are? As much as orcas and humans have lived side by side around the world, why hasn't one case been reported of an orca eating a human if for no other reason than by accident?

It is one thing to say that orcas do not prey upon humans for food, and it is another to say they don't attack humans even in defense of themselves of their young. Time and again, capture efforts in Puget Sound and elsewhere have involved driving orcas into coves where they could be netted, no easy undertaking. In all capture efforts, the orcas have given every impression of being aware that humans are pursuing them and of trying their best to evade capture. Many efforts have failed despite the coordinated use of powerboats, float planes dropping bombs and a half million dollars in expense. But when the orcas are netted and the net is tightened so that individual orcas can be selected and removed from the water, there may be ten orcas packed into one small area. If a female escapes but her baby doesn't she may swim back into the net. And some orcas either charge and break through the net or leap over it, which is unusual because they fear nets so much, probably because nets entangle and drown them.

Amidst the panic, divers enter the water with the orcas, which would seem terribly dangerous, but, oddly, none of them ever have been even slightly harmed. No direct attacks, which of course would prove fatal, not so much as a man being struck by a tail fluke. During some captures, which occurred regularly over ten years in Puget Sound, an orca became ensnared and drowned, but in all these interactions not one human was injured by an orca.

Not only that, but perhaps more astounding, the divers need only swim to an orca, place a hand on its pectoral fin and guide it into a steel cage lowered into the water for removal of an orca. Try to imagine the circumstances: orcas churning the water in a frenzy to escape, but a puny human being swims among them unharmed and with naught but his hand moves a behemoth into a small cage. Orcas that were never netted or which escaped the net are outside breaching, calling and slapping the water over and over again as though protesting human behavior and enticing their fellows to escape.

More than a few of the orcas that entered the lift-cage never survived. They were found dead, drowned in minutes at the bottom of the cage. The divers told me that the orcas submerged, let their air out and quickly died—they say they committed suicide in the cage rather than be taken captive. After fully reviewing all the evidence, including interviews with the men involved and films made by the chief diver during every capture, one can only conclude that in the very circumstances in which orcas would definitely be expected to be aggressive to humans, they weren't. And the possibility that some of them would commit suicide before they would harm a human cannot be ignored, all of orca behavior taken into account.

There is one record at least of an orca attacking a vessel, and the context indicates that the orca was quite aware of what it was doing. It was in Bellingham Bay, northwest Washington, during the earliest effort to capture an orca. A sixty foot long boat netted an adult female orca and a youngster, possibly the female's offspring.

The adult male who seemed to respond to the netted orca's calls, charged the boat at high speed, once, twice, then a third time when the crew shot it in the head and killed it before the boat sank from the damage inflicted by the orca. Unfortunately, the net was pulled down with the

Tlingit killer whale hat.

PHOTO COURTESY OF BURKE MUSEUM, UNIVERSITY OF WASHINGTON

boat and the captives drowned.

There are a couple other reports, less conclusive, that orcas attacked sailing boats at sea, but perhaps it is not the same thing to attack a boat as it is to attack a human body. Still, any way one dissects the data, it is most peculiar that the many orcas netted in Puget Sound never defended themselves or their young with aggressive action against humans so vulnerable and conspicuous. To suggest that the orcas did not perceive their captors as enemies would be stupid. A shark, fox, bobcat, deer, quail, zebra, lion, bear or mouse under comparable conditions would certainly strike out against a human captor. Of course, none of these animals would allow a person to approach and direct it into a cage with nothing more than some gentle nudging. No, the suggestion should be to the contrary: orcas

Beaded neck ornament, Tlingit.

consciously and deliberately avoided harming their captors.

I propose that orcas avoid killing people even in self-defense because they know that the long-term risks from harming humans is too great. Judging from human response to other predators, they would be right. An accidental killing of a human by an orca would mean wholesale slaughter of orcas, though orcas are killed en masse because they compete for fish, as in Norway. The only creature we know that makes such complex cost-benefit analyses is man. Were we in the orca's place, dominated by a clearly superior species against which we could never win in the long-run, our behavior would be no different.

Indeed, our crisis is strictly a problem of preventing short, term failure and maximizing long-term success. Can we inhibit warfare as competition for resources increases? Can we conserve now what we need later? Can humans sacrifice immediate gains for long-term success? It appears that orcas make such decisions positively in relationship to one another, and, if not

Killer whale house, northwest coast.

to other animals, then at least to us, their new found superiors. Perhaps orcas can teach us to cultivate our self-interests so that we can live in the world without destroying it. Maybe we can learn to rule a world without wielding weapons. It's time we come to grips with the lion and wolf inside and devote ourselves to the transmutation required to be more like the orca, at peace with ourselves.

Though the Makah whalers were not dominant to the orca, the orca did not kill them. Neither did the Makah kill the orcas. They killed bears, who occasionally killed them as well, and they also killed the wolf and cougar, as great power symbols, trophies indicating a man's prowess. But when it came to the orca, things were different. A young whaler might ride an orca to prove his worth, and such a daring deed was very much

RANDALL L. EATON

Entrance to graveyard at Alert Bay, British Columbia.

esteemed. But if a young man with harpoon itch can ride an orca, he could also kill one and, ostensibly, collect the ultimate trophy. Why not?

Because the Makah saw in the orca their world's most powerful and intelligent being, a being who neither feared nor attacked them. Men who compete with other predators make of them their gods, because those creatures rule their lives, limit their possibilities, take their food and kill them. And when a man kills his god he takes that god-power into himself. The consequences of winning against predator-gods are not to be measured solely in the realm of the spirit, but practically: a predator-god-trophy earns a man more wives and children, rank and power among men, and altogether greater reproductive success. Natural selection has favored the high-risk strategy of hunting predator trophies because some men win big. Indeed, the only way to explain the human's rise to power over predators—and planetary dominion—is trophyism.

Over time enough men killed their gods to usurp godhead. Their gods ceased being bears and lions and became fashioned after the hunter–warrior. As predators gave way to humans, humans became their own major competitors, the wars began in earnest and the great heroes like Hercules and David replaced the predator-gods, lion and bear. So, in our quest for power our gods evolved from predator to human, and if we are to rule the warrior god it will not be by force but some other gift…inner peace.

The orca was a step above god for a reason: it was one step above man and his projection of himself to godhead. We could never claim power for killing a being whose sense of the sacred places its death above killing us. The Makah whalers were staunch egoists, civilized Indians whose society was structured by warring and trophies, the highest ranking of which were whales because they were most powerful and dangerous. But the Makah saw the orca as this planet's perfect ruler, blessed with what every human wants—freedom. Freedom from strife with one another, and free from conflict with enemies. The perfect dominant struggles not within itself nor against its world. That is the orca. Perfect Buddahood. One step above god…one step above ourselves.

9

Orcas That Kill Humans?

"WE ARE VERY SUPERSTITIOUS about killer whales up here. We know from our ancestors from way back that they once tried to kill a whale like that, a killer whale, and they hardly wounded it. It is known that the whale capsized the boat and chewed up both human beings who were in the boat. It is said that these whales have a good memory and even after many numbers of years pass, they always know which human being had been shooting at them."

So said Raymond T. Aguvlak, an Eskimo, to Erich Hoyt. This day in Barrow when orcas are sighted, loud halers warn all whalers and fishermen to take to shore.

Mere myth? No scientific or "factual" basis? The legends of hunting societies may be trusted to contain some degree of truth precisely because, for them, accuracy is a necessity. Only anthropologists and others who have devoted themselves to the study of hunting societies fully appreciate how tenaciously hunters adhere to the actual events of their lives. It is with agrarian peoples that immensely distorted and superstitious beliefs acquire importance, not with hunters who are always corrected for the smallest error whether their story is personally or socially derived. To hunt is to rely upon receiving, following and transmitting information accurately; otherwise, individuals and their kin make precious errors, conceivably fatal. For us in post-hunting societies, who seem to revel in distortion and gossip, it is hard to imagine the ability with which hunters maintain the same stories over countless generations, but it would take little reintroduction to that way of life for us to rediscover the vitally important origins of culture and story-telling as memory devices.

Look at the Eskimo's killer whale story in this way: were it inaccurate then the Eskimos would be spending much time and energy needlessly avoiding orcas when they might just as well kill them for food. Although in the past six decades the Eskimos have moved from a true subsistence life into dependency on the U.S. government, before that, when the story originated, they did rely largely or wholly on hunting for their survival. In that primal way of living for thousands of years, a false perception of the risks of harming or killing orcas would have cost the people enormously. To leave the water or cease hunting for a while could mean loss of prey and that could mean virtual starvation of a family or larger unit in a harsh world where animal food is premium.

And along with theoretical deduction are the convincing findings of anthropologists such as Richard Nelson who have lived with Eskimos day after day, hunting with them and sharing their life. He found that Eskimo hunters live by accurate observation and story-telling, that braggadocio is non-existent, and that the Eskimos are far better informed with infinitely greater detail about their world and the creatures in it than non-Eskimo scientists who study their world. The same applies to the Kalahari Bushman of southern Africa, the Aborigines of Australia and so on, for every hunting society examined in depth.

So, orcas do attack people? Probably, they have. It is to the story that we now turn for insights.

How, exactly, could an orca in the water know that men inside boats—that is, men *not* in the water—wounded it? If the orca were a blindly instinctive creature, then it would be adapted or pre-programmed by evolution to respond to natural predators in its world, which hardly resemble anything like a skin boat. The orca's enemies probably include sharks, possibly other orcas though we have no evidence to indicate that. Because we know from actual experiments conducted on the sensory physiology of delphinids that they are incredibly well adapted to discriminate things in their world with sonar that penetrates bodies, no one could legitimately argue that orcas could possibly mistake a skin boat for any sea or land creature. And if we allow that the orca somehow knew that his pain from the wound were somehow inflicted by the boat, why didn't it simply attack the boat? Why chew the men inside the boat? Neither the Eskimos nor anyone else who has lived with orcas for centuries or studied them whether through the classics, ethnography, mythology or direct observation has presented any evidence that orcas may prey upon people, i.e. eat them for food.

And if we agree with the plausibility of the story so far, we need also wonder why the wounded orca or others with it didn't attack other boats and men? And if not at the time one orca was wounded then later. Note that the story goes on to say that orcas have a good memory and even if a number of years pass, they always know which human had been shooting at them. The Eskimos may have additional experience not contained within this particular story but embedded elsewhere in their mythomemory that forms a basis for this component. The implication clearly is that on some other occasion someone shot at or wounded or killed an orca, and many years later orcas attacked or killed that same person or persons.

The question then is whether orcas take revenge on humans? Erich Hoyt has discussed this question in his book about *Orca: The Whale Called Killer,*

"The revenge concept makes little sense if one considers the percentage of orcas with bullet wounds found in aquariums or in the waters off the Northwest Coast. Those animals may be a little wary, but their behavior around humans and boats is unthreatening. In fact, the *absence* of revenge is worth discussing: In other mammalian species—elephants, tigers, grizzlies—bullet-wounded individuals sometimes become 'rogues,' man-killers seemingly sworn to avenge their sufferings. But not killer whales, as far as we know."

I think Hoyt nearly hit the mark. He is right to point out that many hundreds of orcas that have been wounded by people have been and are still swimming among humans and boats without taking revenge. But that is not what the old Eskimo story says; it implies something quite specific, and that is that orcas in their area have attacked those particular humans who have harmed them. That orcas may turn "rogue" *only* on certain individuals for certain reasons in certain areas seems to be well worth considering not only because mythological evidence and other information suggest such a possibility, but also because, if factual, we have found another distinct difference between orcas and other rogue-prone species including large carnivores and humans. I say humans because it is quite common for them to take reprisals or revenge not on a particular individual, unless he is within their group, but against anyone of the foreign group held accountable for a theft or killing even when that killing may occur under agreed-upon conditions of war.

And, in the realm of revenge against other species, humans have rarely concerned themselves with getting the culprit. Normally, they do their best to kill any and all members of the species, including, hopefully, the culprit. When it comes to revenge on other species humans seem to uphold the philosophy of an eye for many eyes, and of course, that has been an extremely important aspect of human evolution and rise to dominance. We are excellent erradicators of our enemies, human and non-human, and it is for this reason that our present subject is so interesting and important in this age in which we have come to ponder and doubt our ways, our values and ourselves.

If orcas do kill only culprit humans then, of course, they exercise a quite sophisticated code of conduct in their relationship to humans. Again leaving aside their apparently uncanny ability to discriminate bad people from not-bad people, let us go further into the myth that orcas are vengeful.

An Alert Bay, British Columbia, fisherman told Hoyt a story from his youth. A Kwakiutl Indian man shot an orca and when he towed its body to the beach to show the people, 'No one wanted anything to do with him.' The elders warned the fisherman that, 'The blackfish [orca] will get you,' and when later the man went out fishing and never returned, everyone assumed that orcas killed him. I am not assuming that orcas did in fact kill the fisherman, but I would stress the fact that the Kwakiutls strongly believed that orcas would take revenge on the particular man who had killed one, and I argue that there is a real basis to that belief based on my studies not only of hunting peoples but also their universal myths regarding the threat of certain, really dangerous creatures, the difference here being that consistently we find among the Northwest hunters the belief in revenge being specific to the culprit. *That* is exactly what makes this mythical quality stand out among myths about awesome predators.

The Tlingits of the Alaskan panhandle so feared the orca that some of them refused to go whaling (for species other than orcas) when they were originally contacted by Europeans. That every other Northwest Coastal tribe practised whaling to some degree, and obviously whaling may be a lucrative though risky venture, would suggest that the Tlingit's attitude about orcas has some historical basis in orcas attacking them.

The story still told around Barrow, Hoyt says, is of a North Alaskan Eskimo who harpooned an orca then found orcas waiting for him each time he launched his kayak until he felt forced to abandon the sea altogether. Another story mentioned by Hoyt tells of two young Eskimos who drowned off the

Alaskan coast; one of them had shot at an orca, and the locals attributed the boys' death to that, though the details of how they died were apparently unknown.

A similar story was originally published by Paul Spong in *Mind in the Waters,* and this one was not about Indians or Eskimos but loggers. Two loggers were skidding logs down a slope into the water, and when one of them noticed a pod of orcas swimming by he released a log with the intention of hitting one, and he did, in the back, 'apparently injuring but not killing it.' The whales went away but that evening as the men were rowing their boat back to camp the orcas reappeared and capsized the boat. One man vanished, the one who had sent the log down that hit the orca, and the other man was not harmed and survived to tell the story.

The persistent element in all these myths, Native American or European-American in origin, is that orcas may in certain areas at least attack and kill humans who have injured or killed them. In my essay, Do Sperm Whales Feel Pain When Bombs Explode Inside Their Bodies?, I describe a modern incident of a sperm whale who, when a cow in his herd was harpooned by a Russian whaler, immediately ceased fleeing from the whaler, turned back but bypassed the Greenpeace raft and its occupants and went directly to the bow of the ship and thrust himself straight up out of the water towards the harpooner on the prow who had shot the cow. There is no conceivable way to explain the bull's behavior except to infer that he had full consciousness of who had done what to whom—and he attempted to avenge that fatal deed with unhesitatingly appropriate action.

The same may be said for the male orca who appeared on the scene after a cow orca and her calf had been netted in Bellingham Bay, Washington, with the intention of taking one into captivity. Apparently the male responded to the netted orcas' calls, and in any case he rammed the boat three times before he was shot and killed, though the boat sank and pulled down the net and drowned the orcas in it. Here again, as in the case of the vengeful sperm whale, an orca is taking quite specific action against humans inflicting what surely was perceived by it as harmful.

As for the few claims of orcas sinking boats at sea without apparent provocation, not only do all of them lack substantive sightings of orcas actually striking the boats, no one may really say that the attacks, if they occurred, were unprovoked. Infant orcas are much more vulnerable to all sorts of dangers than are adults, and if a boat were to unknowingly hit a young orca, who knows that adults wouldn't attack the boat? For one thing these boats have been out to sea alone and out of sight of other boats, so, for all we know, orcas make assessments about the relative costs and benefits to themselves of taking revenge on people. Regardless, if orcas have really sunk the boats as survivors claimed, one thing may be concluded for sure: whenever humans were in the water they were *not* attacked.

After reviewing all the evidence, stories, anecdotes and myths, I am certain that orcas have attacked and killed humans, but under quite specific circumstances, and not always under these. I think that the only time they do so is when they have been harmed, and then only when they can take revenge *without* risking a heavy backlash from humans. In those areas such as Puget Sound where humans have been shooting, capturing and sinking orcas for many years, the orcas have not and do not attack humans even in self-defense, though, of course, they easily could. But it's also true that if they ever did attack a human in this region they could pay a very high price indeed; chances are quite high that they'd all be dead soon. But in areas such as southeast Alaska or Eskimoan Alaska, right up to the present day orcas could successfully take revenge against humans *without* paying a heavy price. And, as for incidents at deep sea, if my hypothesis is correct, orcas may attack solitary, smaller craft when they harm orcas.

Not only do the whaling logs convince us that orcas presented no harm to humans in the water with them, they also document the extraordinary cooperation of orcas and humans in whaling.

So, on the one hand we have direct evidence that establishes beyond doubt that: 1) orcas may cooperate with humans; and, 2) orcas may refuse to be aggressive to humans in self-defense or to defend young, as during capture. On the other, we have some kinds of evidence that strongly suggest that: 1) orcas have attacked and killed humans in response to humans harming them; and, 2) these attacks may be highly specific, directed to certain vessels or humans inflicting harm to orcas. There is compelling evidence that orcas have nearly killed humans accidentally, either mistaking them for prey or out of curiosity. That, too, would be expected, but what is so surprising is that none of these accidents have been fatal.

Perhaps we should expect precisely this sort of paradoxical image to emerge for a creature able to make fine discrimination and assessment about the consequences of its actions. What stands out most clearly is that orcas uphold a definite value system when it comes to their interaction and relationships with humanity, and, if I am right here, then their ethical code far surpasses ours. That orcas may attack humans is not a serious blow to my or anyone else's lofty image of them; rather, it would indicate that "they're only orcas," and in their relationship with humans, their ethical code would be absolute and unerring, the proper balance of the golden rule (applied by them to another species, us); literally, the eye that harms for the eye harmed...justice.

If and when an orca kills a human, let's all of us pray that humanity considers its verdict with humility in light of how grossly we have violated them.

P.S. Orcas don't make many mistakes. The orca that leaped through the air and struck and killed a trainer at Sea World apparently did so deliberately. The inside story that emerged upon closer investigation was that the trainer had been using a cattle prod on the orca.

10

Namu and the Orca Nation's Quest for Humanity

T HE EVENTS SURROUNDING THE CAPTURE OF NAMU, first orca ever to live for any period of time in captivity, suggest not only that orcas have a mind of their own, but that they are also capable of perceiving human intentions and deciding for themselves how they will conform with those intentions.

In northern British Columbia, Namu became trapped in a net when he entered it apparently to rescue a young orca inside. Namu guided the calf out through an open flap of the net but Namu remained inside. After Namu had been captured for several days and interacted with orcas of his pod through the net, Ted Griffin arrived to buy Namu and make preparations to transport him to Seattle. During the evening, Griffin left two men in a boat to keep an eye on Namu; for one thing, Griffin feared that some local might try to free him.

One of the men was Don Goldsberry, with years of aquarium and sea experience, and Homer, a highly experienced trainer of marine mammals. At least Griffin and Goldsberry would have to be considered reliable witnesses for several rea-

sons: neither could be described as especially prone to exagger-
ate, and those like myself who know them would probably
judge them to be reasonably accurate, capable observers; neither of these men indicate in person or in writing that they are
of a mind to believe that orcas are very intelligent, though each
one holds them in great esteem and respect; and, if anything,
both are prone to dislike the popular whale movement in all its
dimensions precisely because it has been sympathy for whales
that has complicated their lives—though Seattleites and the
world at large loved Namu, Griffin's "greatest show on earth"
contributed to public sentiments in favor of leaving wild orcas
alone, and it was this attitude that interfered with Goldsberry's
efforts to catch and sell orcas to oceanariums.

In Ted Griffin's own words from his *Namu: Quest for the
Killer Whale,*

Griffin: 'Homer, how is he? Has he eaten?'

Homer: 'Your whale's doing fine. I think he's eating now,
but,' Homer's voice lowered, 'we nearly lost him the other
night.' Griffin: 'What happened?'

Homer: 'The nets were down for several hours, about ten
feet under-water. The whale could easily have gotten away. In
fact we don't know why he didn't.'

Griffin: 'What did you do?'

Homer: 'Don and I stayed right beside him all night. Now
this may sound crazy, Ted, but a couple of times, when it
seemed he was thinking about swimming away, we talked him
out of it. You know, he just backed up a little, away from the
perimeter. I've gotta tell you that's one fine animal. I just hope
you appreciate the opportunity he presents.'

Homer's closing advise to Griffin has its own tragic tale—
Namu's death and Griffin's internal struggles to resolve himself,
including his confusion about how he should have treated this
remarkable creature. A wild orca, described as the dominant
bull of his orca society, stays inside the perimeter of a net that
no longer is preventing his escape? And men's voices sufficient
to keep him there? No scientist who knows both directly and

through theory and literature the behavior of wild animals ever would have predicted Namu's behavior that evening in a cove in British Columbia. I shall not bother here to treat the shallow attempts to account for Namu's unexpected behavior, his apparent decision to remain stationary when he could have escaped. But I must emphasize that *the simple facts of the case speak profoundly for the interpretation that Namu consciously and intentionally chose to be taken captive by Griffin and his colleagues.* Whether Namu could perceive Homer and Don's intentions when they spoke to him, no one may say, but what is beyond dispute here is the fact that reliable witnesses say Namu easily could have escaped, and he did not. Actually, he could have escaped many times over the succeeding days and weeks, and later when Griffin worked with Namu in a netted cove to make a film.

Perhaps Griffin should have subtitled his book: A Killer Whale's Quest for Humanity. By all appearances, Namu captured himself, and as the self-appointed, original ambassador of the orca nation, he went a long way towards capturing our hearts and endearing us to his people. Namu would have left Seattle as happily as he arrived, had human greed not intervened and, ultimately, destroyed his life. Perhaps, had we read Namu's capabilities and intentions, as clearly communicated when he stayed put rather than fled, he would have come into our world, edified us about his kind, led other orcas to make friendships with humans and vice-versa, and the whole problem of whale slaughter and interspecies communication would have been resolved years ago. That this didn't transpire may be owing to one thing: a man's claim to fame and his desire for fortune. Why else put nets around a being who doesn't need them to cooperate with us?

Believing as I do that orcas are able to perceive our intentions and meet our expectations if they so choose, naturally I consider it not unlikely that some orcas commit suicide during capture—they don't want to live in our world—and others enlist themselves willingly, for awhile anyway. Perhaps still oth-

Orca pod in Johnstone Strait, 1986.

ers, like Haida, commit their lives to bridging the orca-human connection. Instead of letting them go after a period of diplomacy that so far means an unpreferred diet, loneliness and terrible living conditions, we should let *them* choose. Offer them the possibility to leave, to stay, to leave and return, but do not pretend they would not or could not choose for themselves. And should some care to stay, let them do it on their own terms, in their splendid way, trusting the outcome. As long as we force some orcas into captivity perhaps the rest will not trust us. Enslaving orcas for profiteering may be what stands in the way of orcas socializing more freely with humans in nature and at the sea-land interfaces. When we are human enough to give them their right to exercise their own decisions then we shall also be capable of interrelating with them most profitably.

11

Orcas and Dolphins
in Captivity

THE EXHIBITION OF DELPHINIDS IN CAPTIVITY has done more to raise concern for cetaceans than everything else put together. Though TV has personalized dolphin characters like Flipper and contributed immeasurably to affection for dolphins and whales, there are millions upon millions of people in North America, Europe, Japan, South Africa and Australia who visit aquariums and become turned on by dolphins and orcas.

It is delightful to know that the world's most popular attraction is not professional football, soccer of basketball, nor the Olympics, nor exploration of space, nor Disneyland/World, but animals. More people in North America go to zoos and aquariums than take in all the college and professional athletic events combined. That says much of importance about man's desire to recover his soul. The animal is central to man's psyche, his origins, and his affections; thus, the zoo is much more than anyone has ever conceived. It is where we humans reconnect with our earthly kin, and where we share the common lament for another time and place. We visit the zoo to be inspired by the beauty, intelligence and wonder of nature. We also go there to know why we feel wistful about being caged with the animals in civilization, which, try as we may to deny it, is destroying us. The caged animal tells us that there is something fundamentally wrong with the way we and they live. So in this virtually religious homage that hundreds of millions of people annually make to the zoo the animal is not only an ambassador of good will for his still wild brethren, he speaks for their dubious condition, for ours, and also for the communal fact of all life.

Aquariums are significantly different than zoos for two reasons: a) the human's perception of the aquatic environment; and b) the nature of the creatures in the aquariums and what, as a consequence, they communicate to humans. When we humans, who are adapted by evolution and culture to live on land, visit an aquarium we perceive it to be a sizable body of water, what might constitute a very large swimming pool for us. If we saw two orca-sized land animals, say elephants, confined to an area the size of a typical aquarium pool used by orcas we might think that these behemoths have very little space. And if we had seen elephants in the wild or read that they often move over hundreds or thousands of square miles in a year then we would certainly wonder how extreme confinement might influence their behavior and needs. But if we were careful observers of elephants in such an environment, we would also notice that they have little to do. Any trees still standing from their natural browsing, would be severely cropped. Often the elephants would be kept by night in a heated barn and chained to the floor in a stall, perhaps separated from other elephants. They would stand there and rock back and forth for stimulation, repeating the rhythmical pattern of walking, abbreviated to the torso and legs—rather like what humans do while running in place. One might wonder why the zoo elephants rarely have babies with them, or why so very few zoos have ever had baby elephants born in them. Or why, occasionally, every few years, one hears of a zoo elephant becoming intractable, aggressive and violent. Any reasonably thoughtful or empathetic person could easily wonder about a lot of the undesirable circumstances for elephants at the zoo, but few aquarium visitors ever see dolphins or orcas exhibiting what is the equivalent of pacing in a zoo animal.

An orca is adapted to move through huge expanses of water on a regular basis. Like elephants they have immense social tendencies and needs, as much, from all indications, as humans. In degree, each of these species has had to cope with the basic problems of all complex societies—finding food, cooperative foraging, protection of infants against predators, competition for limiting resources, balancing conflicts of interest, which exist for societies based on kinship, competition among polygamous males for females and the specter of violent warfare, and so on. An orca spends incredible portions of time and energy to locate, assess and capture food, and to do so they visit different environments which present different kinds of obstacles and demand variable strategies and solutions. Their feeding space is not only more variable in terms of factors like cover, prey species, and the like, it is three-dimensional, fluid and often dark, demanding the use of systematically more complex perceptual and communication faculties.

Contrast what altogether constitutes the most complicated niche occupied by any organism in the world with its life in what is for it something less than a bathtub. Compare living in a society of a hundred dolphins of every sex and age coordinating its cooperative feeding, defense, child-rearing, government, mating life and health in a dynamic, fluid ocean with living in a round, shallow tank with the company of three or four dolphins with nothing to do but make humans happy by repeating the same thing over and over, day in and day out, year after year. No catching of fish, no swimming at top speed or cavorting or playing at will through unlimited aquatic space, no diving deep or harassing sealions or taking human children for tows in friendly harbors, no interaction with other groups of your kind, no cooperative anti-predator tactics, just the same old, easy-to-master job of jumping together through hoops for the enjoyment of enthusiastic onlookers. For the most curious, exploratory, mobile, playful creature on the planet, an aquarium must be very boring indeed.

All the evidence says so. Poor even by zoo standards, the dolphins and orcas have miserable records in captivity: lousy breeding success; much shorter life than in the wild; and, poor health in captivity—a lot of "brain disease." The stress engendered by boredom and lack of emotional needs being met should be nothing foreign to human consciousness in this day and age.

That elephants submit to human domination has never been fully explained; they must consciously submit to human power, perhaps because they recognize that it's in their interest to do so. That their submission is done regrettably is indicated by the occasional rebellion of one, both in zoos and where they are used as beasts of burden. Especially but not exclusively it is the bull elephants that occasionally kill Mahouts in Ceylon or India, or kill or injure keepers in zoos. That elephants don't attack humans far more often is actually a credit to their intelligence, and I mean that literally, besides which it should be mentioned that they are among the very large-brained creatures, right behind the toothed whales and man. That orcas don't attack humans in captivity is all the more remarkable considering their even greater ability to do so, their predatory nature, and their comparatively worse condition.

In 1979, we conducted a survey of the world's aquariums and learned that most aquariums had no more than a single orca. Here we have a large delphinid, with a tremendous repertoire of social expressions and, by inference, needs, being deprived of any social life save that with humans. Many aquariums do not let their personnel enter the water with orcas, which must make matters all the worse for the orcas, who, like the dolphins, seem to do their utmost to interact with humans as social surrogates. I wasn't surprised a few years ago when the male orca in San Diego's Sea World aquarium grabbed hold of the young woman's leg as she was trying to leave the pool after having made a commercial. She had been swimming with the orca for several minutes, and when she started to leave, he placed his jaws over her thigh. When she struggled, he wounded her. Flesh wounds only, the woman required stitches to mend. That the orca wanted her to stay and play with him seems likely; that he wanted to bite and hurt her seems unlikely. After all, had he intended to harm her, she would have had her leg snapped off, or worse. If anything he bit her very lightly; by orca standards, his may have been a love bite, intended perhaps to communicate affection.

Under captive conditions where dolphins are greatly loved, respected and admired, humans relate to them as persons, and enter the water to swim and play with them. In such circumstances the relationship between dolphins and humans is nothing less than beautiful and awe-inspiring, if not entirely incredible. There the humans have no doubt about the fact that they are dealing with creatures very like humans in some ways. And, I think it must be quite natural in these situations for deep, intimate affection to emerge between species, as has been described to me by experts with first-hand knowledge.

Though many human would think that copulation with an animal is immoral, I wonder if intentions of the participants matter? It is one thing, it seems to me, for a boy to explore sex with a sheep in the same way, basically, that a puppy does with another puppy or a pig does with a hole in the fence; it is another for a man to seek out animals strictly for his sexual pleasure; and, it is still another, for a human and an animal to join together physically as an act of love between beings who really do love one another, and for whom sex is a natural expression of that love. When, that is, the animal is a dolphin.

I am *not* promoting sex with animals nor with dolphins, and I admit that I have never had a sexual experience with any animal or dolphin. I am saying that I can conceive how someone might make love with a dolphin. We know this is possible because it has happened.

In a relatively open-minded research setting with dolphins, one male student worked closely with an isolated female. The young man was as much the center of the dolphin's world as she was his. The relationship became a virtual love affair, possible, I must repeat, not because of sex, but because a dolphin and a human are capable of relating as loving beings on the same level. Communion is possible through affinity and affection. The young man became disturbed that he was in love and conducting an affair of the heart, mind and body with another creature, so he left the female dolphin and went away, incapable of continuing his project. Two weeks later, I was informed, the female was found dead in her pool, drowned, apparently by her own devices. Nothing was "wrong" with her save the possibility of a broken heart.

If we pause to make too much out of human/dolphin sex then we shall miss the crucial points: that dolphins are human-like; that they may relate to us in human fashion; that they are loving creatures with social needs; and, that in captivity they live terribly boring, lonely lives.

As I was saying, orcas are even more deprived in the usual aquarium simply because many are alone. That orcas are capable of expressing affection sexually to humans is a fact; that they do so rarely in aquariums suggests that they may understand human disapproval of it.

After Ted Griffin had captured Namu and moved him to Bud Inlet, a cove across from Seattle, and everything had quieted down—the press had gone, the capture crew and friends had left—a most unexpected thing occurred when Ted went down to the water to see Namu. Ted had spent years swimming with orcas in Puget Sound; they were his fascination in life and that was his motive for capturing and showing orcas to the world. While his experience and attitude toward orcas assured him that he had nothing to fear, still, this was the first time he thought about entering the water with a fully grown, bull orca whale he had just made captive. Rather than swim into the cove with Namu he waded in up to his waist. Namu swam to Ted, coming as close as the shallow water would permit, and, rolling onto his side, rubbed his long, erect penis gently against Ted's thigh. Ted was embarrassed to recount this incident, but he knew that despite however bizarre the story might sound, it said something profound about Namu and orcas. Ted felt that Namu was saying in his way that he loved Ted, that he knew Ted cared for him. I think Ted was right.

Orcas have survived about ten years on average in aquariums, no matter how old they are when captured. For reasons I discuss elsewhere, we know that one orca died in the wild at an age of at least 140 years, then by accident. Some estimates run 70 years for males, 100 for females in the wild. That they succumb to disease is not definite. Despite their authoritarian utterings, cetacean medicine men don't know much about whales or their maladies. Disease may result form stress, boredom and loneliness. (One must keep in mind that aquariums are not eager to retain marine mammal veterinarians who point to the conditions of captive life as the cause of whale disease, poor breeding and short life. Neither would most of these specialists want to admit it publicly.)

Breeding success is an indicator of how well a species tolerates captivity. In all the aquariums in all the years that sexually mature pairs of orcas have resided, only four births occurred before 1986, three of these to the same parents, all dead within a month.

The first orca born died from "brain disease," the second and third from God knows what. The parents were quite attentive, and there is no reason to suspect that anything was abnormal about the babies. John Lilly interjected his thoughts after the first baby's death, saying that the parents wanted it to die because they didn't want their baby to grow up in the unfit aquarium environment. Some of the whale enthusiasts were quick to mouth his words. Why, exactly, if the parents didn't want the first baby to survive, did they have a second and a third? And why, if they wanted the babies to die didn't they eat them outright and save themselves and the infants a lot of suffering?

Why wouldn't the infant feed from its mother in the particular aquarium where it was born? Having had extensive experience in contriving environments and social settings to promote the breeding success of species that rarely propagate in captivity, I reasoned as follows. The mother normally would need to move in a fairly straight direction without much horizontal, vertical or lateral movement. To vary her trajectory much would make it difficult for the baby to intercept the ejected milk, especially since, in an aquatic medium, the baby would need to be close to the source of the milk or it would be diffused.

It so happens that orcas feed from their mothers as they move more or less in a direct line of movement, rather slowly, and usually in deep water, well away from the hazards presented by shorelines. The shore itself must present considerable risk to a tiny orca whose relatively small body could be pushed ashore or flung against rocks by strong waves. In other words, one of the least likely places for an orca to feed from its mother would be shallow water, which means that the infant orca should be inhibited from feeding under the following conditions: a) in proximity of a shoreline; b) whenever its mother is moving in any direction or manner other than directly ahead, and because the baby may need to breathe relatively often compared to an adult, c) whenever its mother is not close to or at the surface.

Conditions "a" and "b" existed in the aquarium where none of the infants ever fed from the mother. All the baby orcas did was circle the edge of the aquarium, as though looking for a way out to deeper, safer water. Even if the "shoreline" presented by the aquarium edge were not inhibiting to the infant, its mother could not have induced the infant to follow her in a direction long enough for the infant to feed in its pre-programmed, instinctive fashion. Expecting an infant orca to be able to feed in this aquarium pool would be as stupid as presenting a one-day-old human with milk in a glass and expecting it to consume it. No matter how intelligent or susceptible humans are to learning, they are adapted by evolution to expect certain things in their environments and respond to them in a very definite fashion, the example here being the mother's breast and nipple and the baby's searching and sucking response. And the same principle applies to baby orcas—they come into this world innately expecting to find a mother whose behavior and circumstances signal its very definite feeding behavior.

I wrote the aquarium and shared these ideas with them, but received no response. They were proud of themselves for being the first aquarium in the world to produce an orca—such are the trophies of zoos and aquariums—that they didn't see the need for changing things. (The baby was born despite anything they did short of putting a potential mother and father orca together.) I believe they tried force-feeding the baby orca, but that did no good. That the infant orca needs to receive a special milk with ingredients made only by its mother is probably so, and to my knowledge no one had analyzed orca milk or created an adequate substitute, which could mean that they actually harmed the infant rather than helped it. No doubt, the aquarium personnel wanted those infants to survive, but they did not alter the aquarium conditions to make that possible, nor did they release the mother and infant so it could survive.

From a hard, cold perspective of aquarium owners—most aquariums with orcas are private and incredibly wealthy thanks in large measure to their orcas—it would have behooved them to spend millions of dollars in pool development and expansion solely as a means of encouraging the second infant orca's survival. Why? Because they would have made millions in return owing to the immensely attractive baby orca. The show of shows in the world would have been those parent orcas and their beautiful baby. They could have sought investment for an adequate pool precisely for the purpose of propagating orcas. Irrespective of moral attitudes concerning orcas or their survival and reproduction in captivity, which is a business concern in light of the fact that a single orca may cost a million dollars, they would have made out like bandits for "owning" the darling of all aquariums—a baby orca.

Many public zoos and aquariums suffer from everything that any public facility does—poor management, lack of imagination and creativity, the horrible influence of politics, lack of spirit among employees, and all the rest of it, including waste and inefficiency. On the other hand are the majority of private zoos and aquariums which, despite claims and appearances to the contrary, are after profits. I say this knowing quite well that there are exemplary exceptions on both sides of the coin. Private aquariums may not be expected to sacrifice profits except for the sake of public relations. Their much publicized research programs or financial assistance to projects outside the aquarium itself are geared toward promotion, which is profitable for them, or for knowledge which may help protect their sizeable investment in expensive, hard to acquire animals such as orcas.

Fortunately, I also took considerable effort to communicate to Sea World in 1976 how they might proceed to improve conditions for their orcas, add to their longevity in captivity, propagate them successfully and curtail disease. I emphasized why all this would be profitable. At the time I was in the midst of orca studies in Puget Sound which had been associated with tremendous public disapproval of capturing orcas and placing them in captivity, and I argued that before long it might be impossible to capture additional orcas for aquariums, in which case, their big money maker would be lost, and their profits would plummet accordingly. Even if they could capture orcas in other places than Puget Sound, which they did for a while in Iceland after Puget Sound was declared off limits to them, they had to see the writing on the wall. Sooner or later the public would demand that all orcas, possibly all dolphins, be left in the sea. (I predict that this will happen unless we ruin the seas.)

I meticulously outlined the social needs of orcas—keeping a

group of at least two males and three or four females from wild-living pods. Animals from the same region are already socialized to one another and most apt to interact well in captivity, and if adults, already could have bred. Such a group would provide each orca with "social security," fulfillment of social needs. And they would have to be kept in a pool or series of pools much larger than anything yet constructed in the world, though I urged them to consider developing a naturalistic aquarium.

It would be cheap to net off a bay or cove compared to building a concrete pool with all its expensive support facilities which include filtering systems, and such a setting would offer many of the sources of stimulation normally encountered by orcas in the wild, but not in captivity. Fish would swim into the cove or could be released there for orcas to catch their own food, or some of it anyway. Many tourists could be accommodated at numerous locales in easy access to major cities or travel routes on the east or west coast. Orcas would not have to perform for their dinner, and I am confident that the paying visitors would find a naturalistic situation more rewarding. Imagine walking on a floating boardwalk over a large cove by the sea watching a group of orcas with their young behaving naturally, compared with seeing an orca leap out of a small pool surrounded by concrete and a hundred ways to spend your money.

People prefer driving through a naturalistic wildlife park rather than seeing the same animals in a zoo because of the reversal of the role of animal and human. As Lion Country advertised before ignorance and greed corrupted their success, "The animals are free, the people are caged in their cars." Likewise, people would relish a sense of non-obtrusive intimacy with seemingly free, untamed orcas. No doubt the orcas would befriend people, but no matter how they would interact with human onlookers, the sight and sound of orcas themselves would be highly profitable. Why a counterpart to a drive-through wildlife park does not exist among seaquariums is a mystery; one with orcas, dolphins, and other sea mammals, would be a gold mine.

Sea World did not opt for a marine park, but they did decide to enlarge their pools, capture several adult orcas and put them together as a group in their largest pool at Orlando for the purpose of breeding. Having been driven out of Puget Sound, then Iceland, they knew they had better do something or they wouldn't be in orcas and profits for long.

In 1985 an orca was born. Able to feed from its mother in the largest aquarium in the world, it was the first to survive in captivity. Months later, the TV program 20-20 aired the events including the coaching by human wetnurses, the actual birth and the infant's behavior. It was the most inspirational animal show I've seen, and I eagerly await the day when I may meet the "first born." (I like thinking of her as my step-daughter.) With proper care and wise management, that baby orca may become an ambassador for the orca nation, and more. Hopefully, its birth indicates the cessation of orca captures on the one hand, and the building of an intimate bridge between them and us on the other. Orcas are the world's leading attraction, and she became the most popular of orcas.

I wish Sea World would feed the orcas live fish so as to let them exercise in the proper manner as predators, a level of stimulation they may need. When we meet the natural needs of orcas we not only improve their health, we also make them more interesting to the public. From a research point of view, observations of orcas using communication to catch fish would be illuminating.

Imagine what the consequences would be if someone began to talk to an orca at Sea World? What if, for example the orca said it wanted to return to the sea, to be free? That could be the end of Sea World's profits, which brings us full circle back to the problem of self-interests: if the salvation of wild orcas, dolphins and other whales, possibly even the sea, were enhanced by deciphering orcanese, and humans could talk to them, the profiteers would perceive such a revolutionary breakthrough as a threat to their wealth. Profits and enlightenment don't mix when the latter must be given up for the former. In short, that beautiful baby orca is alive for one reason, Sea World's profits, and for that reason its prospects for contribution to human-whale relationships dubious.

Lilly and I agree on the short-sightedness of commercial aquariums regarding openness to scientific research. They fear poor publicity that could result from public knowledge of the abominable conditions and care received by most cetaceans in captivity. Basically the same could be said of most commercial zoos. Overall, scientists could immeasurably improve aquarium conditions and operations in ways beneficial to the commercial interests of the aquariums, the visitors and the whales. Zoo standards have improved dramatically in the past twenty years due to a combination of increasing public interest in animal life and welfare, and increasing behavioral research in zoos.

My experience in aquariums indicated that the major obsta-cle is ignorance of the behavioral adaptations and needs of captive cetaceans, and too great an emphasis and trust in veteri-nary medicine, which, being so ignorant of cetacean biology and behavior, may kill more creatures than it aids. The real progress made in the health and medical treatment of wild ani-mals in captivity has not come through advances in the traditional veterinary sciences such as anatomy, physiology or treatment but in behavioral understanding, which includes nutrition. I made these same criticisms of zoos, and though that meant ostracism by some of the old guard zoo directors, time has proved me right: the leading wild animal medicine specialists would agree that prevention of disease from accom-modating behavioral needs of organisms has meant the most progress in zoos, and the same is possible for aquariums if they or the public expect the much needed improvements.

12

Should We Capture
More Orcas?

I N 1983, SEA WORLD WANTED TO CAPTURE ORCAS. Having already been ousted from Washington State and Canada, as well as Iceland, Sea World set its mark on Alaska. It sought official permission from the Marine Mammal Commission to capture a hundred and keep ten. The company said it wanted to capture so many to collect data on social behavior and physiology. Ken Balcomb, a specialist in photo-identification of orcas, would collect information on pod membership, and others would collect tissue samples. Ten of the orcas would be kept for Sea World's aquariums and propagation.

Hearings were conducted in Seattle. Protests included accusations that the captures themselves could be socially disruptive, and based on the capture team used by Sea World previously in Puget Sound, downright harmful. The same capture experts had killed orcas accidentally, and worse, they had hidden the deaths by sinking the orcas. Collection of tissues for establishment of physiological normals of orcas, conceivably useful to Sea World in health management, may have been questioned for the simple reason that samples from frightened, stressed orcas would be abnormal.

The Marine Mammal Commission was reputed to claim that the Sea World proposal was the most complete they had received. Despite vehement protests from Greenpeace, The Whale Museum on San Juan Island and other preservation and research groups, the Commission granted the permits.

Sea World launched a huge publicity campaign that included full-page ads in newspapers asking people in favor to write the state government. That they did alright, but the tally was about nine to one against removal of orcas from the state. The Governor at the time insisted that Sea World would be able to capture and keep orcas despite overwhelming disagreement by the public, and a political battle ensued.

I became tangentially involved in the conflict by sending out publicity about the orcas killed during capture efforts, which I had documented from personnel involved. From my point of view, Sea World had had seven years to make radical improvements in its aquarium facilities and care of orcas. To this day orcas at Sea World and other aquariums have a short life-expectancy, and though Sea World had begun to enlarge its pools to enhance propagation, they were then as now consumers rather than producers of orcas. A few births hardly offset the dozens of orcas' lives that have been given over to their profits. I suspect that had Sea World been assured of being able to continue capturing orcas, as in Iceland, they would have elected to do that instead of investing in larger pools and propagation as a source of orcas.

In discussions with the President of Sea World, a man with no training or professional experience of cetaceans, whose office is in New York City, I threatened to go public with films of dead orcas being sunk by the same capture team that Sea World wanted to use in Alaska. He explained to me with the precision of a lawyer that these men were not employees of Sea World, but merely contractors. Which, he said, relieved Sea World of any illegalities.

Regardless, the good citizens of Alaska managed to stop Sea

World, so perhaps now they will be forced to do the very best they can for their remaining orcas' health and breeding success. Without alternative sources of orcas from nature, it's in Sea World's interests to do now what I and others felt they should have done all along. My point is quite simple: if they had really cared about orcas themselves, and had sunk much more of their profits back into their health and reproduction, they wouldn't now be facing the possibility of becoming orcaless— and profitless—in the years ahead. Greed has a way of teaching hard lessons.

I do hope that their orcas live long, healthy lives, hopefully happy as well, but I wonder what will be the consequences of successful breeding? On the positive side, sustaining populations in aquariums via propagation would mean cessation of captures in nature, a benefit to the wild orcas. As for the impacts of captive orcas on human perception of cetaceans, there are many who feel that the orcas have already done enough. Certainly captive orcas have elevated human awareness, and indirectly, the welfare of cetaceans in general. However, orcas are still slaughtered en masse by the Norwegians, and the Japanese still kill and eat them. With nearly thirty years of exhibition as the world's most popular creature, would continued exhibition improve the situation?

For fifteen years, Canadian cetologists have pushed for a compromise between the interests of aquariums and those of orcas. They propose that after a tenure of a year or two in captivity, orcas be returned to their native groups. Had aquariums such as the one in Vancouver abided with this humane solution, I suspect that the public at large would support periodic capture and return of British Columbia's orcas. Instead, the Vancouver Aquarium has taken heat for the death of beloved orcas such as Skana, and they are acquiring new orcas from Iceland, rather than their own backyard, a far more expensive proposition. (Their Icelandic orcas died.)

More attractive yet would be a naturalistic marine park in which orcas have much more space to live in sea-water where they can feed naturally, as on salmon. An entire pod would be captured at a time and kept for a year, then released. This orca attraction would surpass anything yet in public appeal, in terms of research and education, and if managed right, profits.

A progressive step would be giving the orcas their choice between captivity and freedom. The notion is not entirely far-fetched, for example, Namu opted on more than one occasion to remain in captivity; he also seemed to want to leave before his death, but wasn't presented with the opportunity.

The ultimate orca exhibit is the most acceptable: establishing situations in orcaland where people may observe and directly experience wild orcas. Now that Seattle's waterfront has been cleaned up, why not establish artificial salmon runs for orcas? Until recently, orcas frequented Seattle's waterfront so it would be easy to attract them to a specific locale. When the salmon are not running, fish could be released from tanks where they're raised, and visitors could be assured of seeing orcas daily or weekly or on whatever feeding schedule would be established. The Vancouver and Victoria areas could have similar situations. The orcas would be free, friendly, and regularly accessible. Considering how severely we have depleted their food supply, they could use the extra salmon.

To prevent them from becoming wholly dependent upon human handouts, feeding would need to be interrupted periodically, perhaps during the slow tourist season. Underwater signals could be used to attract the orcas from near and far. This situation offers research and education opportunities that exceed aquariums or marine parks. It would mean that interactions between orca groups could be observed, for example, while also relating orca behavior directly to the orca's environment.

There are alternatives for conveniently connecting humans with orcas or dolphins without diminishing the respect, freedom or health that these admirable beings deserve. Anything less is also an attack against human dignity.

the fifty-ninth whale

their flukes slap spasmodically against the surf
and relentless shrieks fill the air
as a hulk of a man, vigorous but bent from age races against the
black wind of an incoming storm
his strength waning with each expert lunge of the lance
deep into the jugular

the rising tide whips the bloodsoaked sand
into a purple froth
as he lances the fifty-eighth whale

who else would do it, he wonders
and why, of all people, should he be the one—he who knows better
than to pause and look in their eyes
those godlike eyes that follow his every move and thought begging
for a mercy only he can deliver

drained, exhausted
dreading those penetrating eyes
he sits beside the last dying whale pondering what he's done
and hears a faint cry

that female down the beach
the one his lance couldn't reach
between the wave-tumbled corpses surrounding her
she's crying, crying outloud to no one but him

it's dark now
he's bone tired, numb
couldn't kill her if he wanted, he thinks,
so he trudges up the bank to his cottage
and collapses in a deadman's sleep
until she beckons him hours before daylight

stumbling from bed, he gulps a cup of cold, strong coffee
grabs the lance and heads to the beach
wondering if she's already dead
maybe it was a dream, perhaps by some miracle,
the kindness of a seagod,
she was taken back in a great wave
but just when he is sure he should have stayed in bed
he hears her pitiful cries from the shore below

crawling over giants washed up like logs in the storm
he stands knee deep in the pool carved by her futile gape
her entire body shudders at the touch of his face and arms
pressed tight against her

with one powerful thrust he cuts her fast and deep
and for him she dies silently
for him she dies in silence

—randall eaton

13

Whale Strandings as 'Burial,' Suicide and Interspecies Communication

IT IS PERPLEXING THAT WHALES SWIM ONTO BEACHES. Many but not all strandings result from whales actually placing themselves on the beach to die. Human intervention normally has no influence: dolphins and whales towed off the shore into deeper water typically strand themselves again, sometimes repeatedly. The explanations for whale strandings have been rather feeble, and though the "causes" may be numerous, no one has addressed the most basic question: Of what possible advantage could there be to a whale in dying ashore rather than at sea? By viewing stranding behavior as a form of burial practise in which the beach is the whale's gravesite, strandings make sense.

The nearly universal tendency to bury or cremate human dead may have originated from the advantages of controlling disease and dangerous predators. Carcasses are scavenged readily by almost all predators such as bears, wolves, lions and hyenas, and these species are also potentially dangerous to humans and their livestock or game resources. By placing corpses underground *and* concentrating them at one location

Mass stranding of sperm whales.
School children inspecting stranded sperm whales (inset). COURTESY *DAILY TELEGRAPH*, NAPIER

away from home or usual haunts, humans can control disease and discourage dangerous or competing predators. Just as a kitten learns to identify mice as prey by first feeding on dead mice brought by its mother, lions which feed on dead humans are more apt to attack living humans. Burial tends to discourage predators from feeding on dead humans and thereby reduces the frequency of attack on living humans.

The same novel idea seems applicable to cetaceans. Cetaceans do have enemies, for example, sharks, which attack youngsters, and if not healthy adults, then injured or disabled adults. Of course, sharks commonly eat dead whales. A dying or dead whale can provide many meals for a lot of sharks in the ocean, and this feeding experience might provoke future attacks against healthy whales or their offspring. If a whale were likely to die, then it would be adaptive for it to strand itself to prevent sharks from eating its body. The mere removal of so much shark food would help the dead whale's surviving kin by lessening the probability of shark attacks on them, not to mention that it would deprive potentially dangerous enemies of much food.

This "burial" concept may explain strandings by individuals and by groups. If only one or a few individuals of a group were inflicted with a dangerous communicable disease or parasite, then it could be adaptive for all members of the group to commit suicide. Humans and animals of many species are known to sacrifice their lives in favor of the lives of others, usually their kin. Whole groups of humans inflicted with a fatal disease or facing a superior enemy have committed suicide to prevent spreading the disease or the enemy from gaining advantage over survivors. Mass suicide may be adaptive for whales, which, by removing their inflicted bodies from the water reduces transmission of disease to unexposed kin.

Whales and dolphins also strand themselves for protection against the most dangerous marine predator, the orca or killer whale. Though land is the only place safe from attack by a pack of orcas, being stranded is itself very dangerous, often causing death. Some stranded whales get off shore at high water, but the risk of injury or death is usually great. We may think of stranding as a last resort escape tactic against dangerous marine predators, and if the fleeing whale does die on shore as a result of stranding itself, at least its enemies have gone hungry. Ultimately, the dead whale, who probably would have died anyway had it not stranded, may benefit its surviving relatives.

Few of the many theories of whale strandings are mutually exclusive, and more than one may apply in a given instance. Most commonly accepted among scientists is the view that a diseased or injured whale strands itself, and some mass strandings are associated with the apparent group leader being sick. Ample evidence indicates that indeed disease and stranding are correlated, but in many cases the disease itself does not account for stranding. When a whale suffers from infestation of parasitic worms in its inner ear, which may disrupt its balance, and then proceeds to strike its head against rocks as though trying to extricate the worms or relieve irritation, the worms do not explain the whale's subsequent behavior of swimming onto the beach directly and by all appearances purposefully. "Burial" on land to prevent communication of disease or sharks from being encouraged to attack survivors does explain stranding. By the same token, the confirmation that one pilot whale of a large group which strands itself was dying, possibly from disease, can not explain why the healthy individuals accompanied the dying one to shore. There may be true leadership in the social organization of cetaceans, but it could never be so faithfully blind to explain mass strandings. In some cases, the entire group dies from stranding despite human intervention, and in others the group leaves of its own accord after one individual dies. This pattern makes sense only if we assume that in mass death from stranding, one or more whales carry a highly communicable disease which may be controlled only by leaving the sea en masse, and that when the group accompanies a dying individual but leaves the shore after it dies, communicable disease isn't responsible for a death. Which then suggests that these creatures are cognizant of death and pay homage to a dying member...burial rites? Descriptions of such behavior indicate that the dying whale goes further ashore than its group members which cluster around the dying individual but in shallows subject to tidal inundation. In other words, the dying animal seems to be placing itself on land while the others semi-strand themselves in apparent anticipation of returning to the sea.

Recent correlation between sites of strandings and reversals of magnetic fields in the earth's crust do *not* mean that disorientation *causes* strandings. It does suggest that some cetaceans, for example pilot whales, employ magnetism to navigate. The scientist who drew the correlation also noted that the whales had empty stomachs, and he proposed that they had become stranded *after* being disoriented for several days offshore, during which time they had not fed. Once they had reached the level of starvation and weakness, they stranded *themselves.* Here is a stroke of brilliance, which, however, still failed to grasp the unifying aspect of strandings. That unifying thread is the stranding itself, the fact that the whales *choose* to die out of the water on land (with one exception, escape from marine predators). The correlation actually supports my hypothesis since, once disoriented and starving, whales would be expected to go ahead and strand themselves.

The most widespread opinion of nonprofessionals about strandings is that they are suicidal demonstration or protest intended to evoke human sympathy for the plight of whales. Interpretation of mass strandings as a sacrificial statement is, of course, ignored or negated by cetologists. That this response is a projection of human values—how we humans might behave were we in the whales' circumstances—in no way discounts its validity. The *fact* that humans could behave similarly actually gives credence to the perceived motive of whales. Most scientists fail to see that their theories about the world are pure human projection; indeed, science is wholly anthropomorphic.

In the face of an unconquerable, aggressive enemy, the best strategy would be a succession of tactics: 1) avoidance of the enemy; 2) subordination or appeasement, but definitely not resistance; 3) cooperation if possible; and, 4) self-sacrifice if it might benefit surviving kin. Humans have behaved these ways, sometimes, apparently, with ultimately greater success of survivors.

We are the indisputable enemies of whales. Not so long ago when we were marginally superior, some whales fought back, as against whalers. But as our dominance became complete, defense by whales largely disappeared, and avoidance became the rule. The cooperation extended by dolphins to humans is well known. What about suicide then as a means of appealing to human sympathy? Is such a theory plausible? It is a *fact* that mass strandings have had the effect of evoking much human sympathy, and by all measures, it would appear that prospects for survivors have improved. Regardless of the conscious awareness or intentions of sperm whales, their strandings seem to have been adaptive in reducing human predation.

Conclusion? We have none. Science never knows or concludes anything with certainty; it is entirely a matter of the hypothetical, that which is *possible*. Considering that sperm whales have the largest, most complex brains ever to evolve on this planet, we would be foolish not to wonder what they really may know. We can at least pursue the possibility of mutual awareness, communication, understanding and benefit. The human condition requires an openness to all possibilities.

14

Rethinking
John Lilly

L IKE ALL GREAT HUMANS on whose shoulders we stand,
John Lilly took on a great trophy, the brain of the dolphin.
So impressed was he with it that he came to discover the dolphin itself, and he quit collecting dolphin brains, a decision indicative of his humanness. The trophy club called science caste him out for his blasphemy: the notion that dolphins are conscious, intelligent beings with whom we might be able to communicate linguistically. Lilly stands out more than ever as the genuine prophet. Intellectual altruists constitute a rare and always endangered lifeform.

I helped assemble speakers from around the world for a scientific conference of importance to the future of whales. Just before the summer of 1980, the International Whaling Commission sent me a copy of the program for this meeting on the Intelligence and Behavior of Cetaceans and the Ethics of Killing Them. I was upset to see that Lilly had not been invited, and circulated the following comments to the list of invited speakers:

"There is much to say of this man John Lilly; indeed, the

calling of this IWC conference to consider the behavior and intelligence of whales and the 'ethics of killing' them is the perfect commendation of Lilly and his courageous vision. Since the IWC meeting is professional at the core, it is more than a commendation, it is a reprieve. That Lilly was not invited to this momentous conference, the ultimate origin of which can be traced only to him, is tragic and speaks to the very narrowness of professional scientific vision against which Lilly has had to struggle too long. By turning his ideas toward non-professionals, Lilly has influenced the public concern and interest culminating in this meeting. We thank you, John Lilly."

It turned out that Lilly was invited after all, and he participated. I didn't.

To recognize the immense influence of a person's vision and courage in shaping our lives is not to accept all that that person believes or says. I disagree much with Lilly and believe there is a lot to add to his basic ideas and method. Though tackling his ideas about cetacean mentality, I uphold and reinforce his popularized view that cetaceans need to be understood and preserved. On this we agree, and except for the sportiveness of genuine science, this is no mere intellectual duel.

My thoughts are responses to Lilly's summary of his research and thoughts about the possibility of interspecies communication with dolphins, *Communication Between Man and Dolphin* (Crown, New York, 1978).

Toni Lilly, John's wife, says in the Prologue that John was "the first person to propose that dolphins are as intelligent as men." The ancients perceived dolphins as level with humans in intelligence. There are comparable examples from wherever humans lived close to dolphins, for instance, in the classical literature of antiquity, not merely western but also Chinese and Arabic. Likewise for ethnography. The Northwest Pacific coastal Indians believed that the orca was one step above god, and similar views persist from the Arctic to the South Pacific. Micronesian fishing societies usually never kill dolphins or whales, and consider them good luck. The Maoris of New

Zealand believe that dolphins are godlike, that they may communicate with humans psychically and in dreams. And even Aristotle shared the Greek view of dolphins having language.

Why humanity lost such perception of delphinids is a question worth much inquiry since it addresses the whole stigma of modernity: much know-how, little know-why.

Why not the Beluga?

TONI LILLY'S WONDERFUL EXPERIENCES swimming with a beluga whale prompts a question about Lilly's choice for interspecies communication research. According to John Lilly's logarithmic scale of brain to body weight the beluga compares favorably to the human, orca and sperm whale, relatively, the largest brained creatures. Moreover, the beluga is widely accepted as the most vocal of cetaceans. Though Lilly found that dolphins can imitate patterns of human speech, a major obstacle to interspecies communication with dolphins has been that their imitations are either ultrasonic or difficult for humans to perceive in "real" time. That is, without adjusting the frequency of dolphin sounds down to the level of human audition. Thus, opportunity for immediate communication between dolphins and humans necessitates technological mediation.

Lilly tried to develop the technology for instantaneous conversion of high frequency emissions from dolphins to the normal hearing spectrum of humans (via the music industry, appropriate technology already may have been available and for much less cost than Lilly's machinery). Since we discovered that a beluga can imitate human speech in real time, wouldn't the beluga be a logical choice for interspecies communication? I raise this suggestion not only to direct further inquiry but also to unveil what I believe has been the major weakness in Lilly's thought about whale mentality and interspecies communication—a lack of deduction from the theory of natural selection.

Selective Thinking

LILLY DOES REFER MUCH to the evolutionary record—how long, for instance, delphinids have been relatively large-brained—but he does not make predictions based on natural selection as a principle of evolution. His writing reflects a lack of awareness of progress during the late 1960s and 70s in animal behavior and ecology. Had he been armed with the precisely penetrating power of evolutionary behaviorism, it seems possible that dolphin intelligence would have become widely accepted in science, and perhaps communication with some cetaceans already would have been commonplace. But he was not, and although millions of people already believe in talking "Flipper," science largely resists the possibility. The majority of the rather paltry scientific funding for study of dolphin and interspecies communication has been awarded to scientists with a physiological or psychological specialty rather than the ecological-ethological-evolutionary types whose broader perception should be more favorable to progress. Essentially, I'm arguing that Lilly is correct overall, but that there are even superior theoretical reasons to support his ideas.

Trained as a physician in neurophysiology, Lilly wouldn't have been exposed to natural selection as it applies to animal and human behavior. Instead, his work remained largely at the level of descriptive and manipulative (correlative) neurology. Lilly was fascinated by the dolphin's brain, but also lost in it, as it were.

Some thinkers including Leo Szilard, Gregory Bateson, Ashley Montagu and Carl Sagan, have either linked up directly with Lilly and his dolphin work or endorsed the direction of his research, but altogether Lilly has not succeeded at promoting his ideas among scientists. Any original thinker is apt to meet much resistance from the established order, and it is no fault of Lilly's that he has a popular following. The degree to which Lilly fell behind scientific investigation of delphinid behavior is indicated in his book which fails to mention many pertinent studies published in foremost scientific journals. He as much as admits that he "dropped out" of dolphin study from 1968 to about 1977, and that meant losing touch with progress in the field and ignorance of several on-going field studies of delphinid behavior and communication important to his thesis. Rather than integrate his earlier neurological/psychological work with the more recent studies of dolphin social behavior, sensory physiology, learning psychology and so on, Lilly turned his attention to construction of complex computer machinery as the technique for interspecies communication.

My point is simply that Lilly's thought and work have consistently centered on physiology and technology, ranging from implantation of electrodes in dolphin brains to a million-dollar computer supposed to aid interspecies communication. It didn't work. If it had, Lilly said that he would take his ingenuous gadget into a natural setting to test it further. We may forgive Lilly for having manipulated dolphin brains; after all, he saw the light, but he proclaimed that it was unethical to confine dolphins for any reason, including research. But where were John Lilly and Project Janus? Marineland, Redwood City, California, experimenting with dolphins. Lilly's thoughts, like his actions, are inconsistent. Perhaps that is not a radical problem, but what about the other end of the spectrum of scientific investigation of delphinid behavior, where observation is made in natural settings, where the adaptive uses and roles of communication present themselves, where dolphins have the latitude to teach us, as they did Jan Doak when she entered the water prepared to meta-communicate with dolphins?

Know Thy Animal

THE MOST BASIC DICTUM OF ETHOLOGY is KNOW THY ANIMAL. Of course, knowing an animal is not only possible in captivity, in some ways it is superior to field study because of the continuity of relationship between scientist and animal, also the intimacy, which is why ethologists believe in both approaches. The advantages of captivating animals for closer observation or experimentation do not necessarily apply to dolphins who make friends with people in the wild. At Monkey Mia, Australia, for example the same dolphins appear like clockwork on beaches to associate with humans.

If we are ever to communicate linguistically with dolphins then it is crucial that we understand how and why they communicate. How do they use communication in social interactions, in hunting, defense against predators? Though there is a valid need for study in captivity as in controlled experiments and for developmental inquiries, these may be done in nature or under semi-natural settings for the sake of the dolphins and observing the spectrum of their behavior. Otherwise we may never acquire the key to the nature of dolphin communication, how it evolved and its structure.

I suspect that Bateson was right, that dolphin communication is not language as we know it, but he was also right in arguing in the first place that human language is a feeble form of communication. Dolphins may be able to conform with our expectations to use some common language system, as Lilly predicts, but in doing so they may not employ their communicative faculties, and that concerns me. I want to know how they communicate with *their* communication system, and then, if possible, simulate and use it to communicate with them. A major shortcoming of Lilly's work is simply that it has contributed little of accurate description of what dolphins do; clearly, the essential task is to understand them and their behavior, much less their brains or interfacing computer technology.

Brains Are Not Intelligence

LILLY'S INTRODUCTION IMMEDIATELY GOES BEYOND the preliminary writing in asserting that whales, "with huge brains are more intelligent than any man or woman." While it is reasonable to infer that large-brained cetaceans are *possibly* as or more intelligent than humans, the problem ignored by Lilly is what constitutes intelligence. And how should we compare species? It would help to clarify his argument if he were to refer the reader to those actual studies that virtually equate human and dolphin mental capacities, such as memory and certain kinds of learning. General intelligence may be immeasurable, it certainly is not the same as brain size or complexity, though it may correlate with these, and, besides, ethologists have for decades pointed out that each species has its own adaptations to its particular environmental circumstances which constitute intelligence in those circumstances, not others. Some insects are capable of certain kinds of learning and problem solving which, under the same conditions, humans would perform less well. Intelligence is not a super-structure of evolution which leads from simple to complex, lower to higher, but a matter of adaptation to environments exploited by different lifeforms. There is no other valid measure of what it means to be intelligent, and that is why we should ask questions about what natural selection has favored in dolphins living in their world. Not, how large are their brains?

Lilly quickly relates his beliefs in cetacean intelligence to the crisis of human survival. He says that we need a new ethic that would incorporate species "with brains comparable to and larger than ours," meaning whales. Not only does Lilly tend to equate, rather than correlate, brain with mentality or intelligence, he fails to tell us why it is in our interest to give large-brained organisms the same rights as other humans in society. As John Eisenberg reminded me when I phoned him to report incidents of orcas imitating human sounds, brain-size in itself is no criterion for justification of protecting anything.

This is the difference between the way a brain man and an ecologist look at the world: the former thinks that the brains have it all, the latter knows that the big-brained beings are no more important to the health of the biosphere and its ability to support life than the brainless creatures. If we were to extend Lilly's ethics out to their logical limit, then we might give priority to saving the relatively large-brained tiger over its relatively small-brained prey species, but that would only jeopardize the existence of the tiger. The microorganisms that make up soil on which all human life depends surely deserve as much right to existence as everything else above them in the pyramid of life. Braininess has nothing to do with ecological ethics; it merely projects human values.

Which brings us to a startling revelation: Lilly is an idealist, his plea for protection of cetaceans pious idealism, which would equate large brains to high intelligence and intrinsic value or worth. Lilly is not alone. Many intellectuals unconsciously project their function in society onto the world, but the fact is that humans do not live for intellect, rather, intellect serves life. This is ratio-vitalism, Ortega's philosophy, which places ego in its real, interdependent relationship with the world.

Lilly begins to justify his claims for cetacean intelligence based on brain size by reviewing the modern history of comparative neurology, but he never tells us why brain study should be central to the question of interspecies communication. Look at the issue this way: do we require knowledge of brains to communicate among ourselves or with other species? Isn't it true that we can know something about how our minds function, as via introspection, without any knowledge of brains? Moreover, has any human advanced the capability of his mind by knowledge of brains? Would precise knowledge of Einstein's brain improve someone's capability as a thinker? Only if comparative study of brains is approached from the perspective of adaptation is it valuable, and its value lies more in what the brain implies about a species' adaptations than in what we may learn from the brain itself. At best, correlative brain study provides gross predictions about what, in general, a lifeform is adapted to do and its potentialities. The neurological predictions have been upheld: most studies indicate advanced mentality in delphinids. But these contributions move us not one step closer to dolphin communication.

Why Big Brains Evolve

LILLY'S NEUROLOGICAL HYPOTHESIS, that the large brains of dolphins mean high intelligence and advanced communication, rests upon his argument that as body-size increases, brain size need not increase in direct proportion. Lilly argues that smaller bodies impose certain physical limitations on brain-size expansion, but he does not say why many large-bodied species have small brains or why a few large-bodied species have relatively much larger brains. Mechanical considerations aside, Lilly says, "The evolutionary selective pressures for and against survival of large brains are not yet fully understood." Generally, however, brain evolution is believed to correlate with the adaptive value of increased learning capacity or the plasticity of behavior and diversity of lifestyles (breadth of niches, exploitation of variable resources, etc.). The advantages of information storage—memory; information sharing—cooperation, communication and culture; and, simulation—the enhanced capability of solving problems at the imaginary level, may account for brain development.

If we overview brain size relative to body size (by any of several indices which make non-linear adjustments) we find that predators tend to have relatively larger brains than their prey of comparable body size. Lions and wolves, for instance, have relatively larger brains than either zebra or deer. The greater importance of learning, including culture, and simulation (mental prediction) to predators explains their larger brains. Neither is it surprising that predators who coexist with dominant, dangerous competitors, such as the margay cat that is sympatric with the larger ocelot, would have relatively a larger brain than its closely related enemy; the smaller predator would have to handle a greater array of survival problems than the similar, larger predator, and this principle no doubt applies to human evolution and that of the beluga, which is preyed upon by humans, orcas and polar bears. Nor is it unexpected that among the larger carnivores the bears have relatively larger brains since, though less social than the lion or wolf, they have the most plastic lifestyle, ranging from predation on large prey and fishing to scavenging from grouped predators, and a wide range of tactics for foraging on vegetation and small mammals. Brain evolution may be related to ecological pressures for cetaceans, too.

Among the cetacea, there is the same, general correlation between brain size and ecological niches (ways of making a living): predators have larger brains; for instance, the Ondontoceti or toothed whales, which include the delphinids as well as the beluga and sperm whale. The baleen whales, on the other hand, are relatively small brained and they are more herbivorous—and, if not really herbivores in the strict sense, at least they forage like herbivores, certainly not like predators. The relationship between the grey whale and its predator, the orca, is analogous to the relationship between bison and the (now extinct) plains wolf, or the Cape buffalo and the lion, or, for that matter, between humans and their traditional prey; in each example, the predator is relatively larger brained.

This is the proper place, then, to dispel the notion that all cetaceans are relatively large-brained, and that whales in general should be highly intelligent or capable of language-like interspecies communication with humans. The brains and the vital problems faced by the toothed whales are far more complex than those of the non-toothed whales. Compared to a dolphin or beluga, a minke whale should be a dunce.

Human and Whale Evolution

BRAINS SHOULD CORRELATE WITH BEHAVIOR, and by either measure it is the toothed cetaceans that are, by far, the most intelligent and communicative. Lilly's logarithmic plot of brain to body size shows dolphin, man, orca and sperm whale as among the most advanced species on earth. These species are predatory by nature. Scientific theory, bodies of evidence and plain old common sense ought to convince anyone that humans are predatory at the core whether or not they eat meat in contemporary civilization.

It was only recently that humans achieved full dominance over their carnivore enemies, and it is clear that dominance was the condition responsible for intense competition among groups of humans which has meant thousands of wars. Despite all appearances, the underlying motive for warfare is always the same: competition for resources ranging from land and women to wealth and armies. The crisis we now face is one of adapting to our own dominance and strategies of competition that brought it about. To realize sufficient cooperation among humans is to cope with previously adaptive competitiveness. The highest ranking toothed whales, the orca and sperm, seem to have solved the major problems that confront a species with dominant status, and this, I believe, is among the most important justifications for studying their behavior and communicating with them.

Of all the toothed whales, the basic social structure of the bottle-nose dolphin most resembles that of primal humanity: a society composed of groups of adult males and larger groups of females and their dependent young. The sperm whale society is somewhat different. The basic society consists of a group of females and offspring, and, often adult males are found either singly or in male groups. Much of the time, males do not accompany groups of females, a situation like that of the largest terrestrial mammal, the elephant, which is also large brained.

With respect to way of living, the human shows much overlap with the orca. Both are fundamentally adapted to prey upon a wide range of species, but especially *large* prey. Dolphins in groups could kill sea mammals for food; however, dolphins would then have to contend with the larger, more formidable orcas. If dolphins were to compete for the same sea mammal resources as the orca, orcas would not only prey upon dolphins for food, as they do, they would also attack and kill them as competitors.

The situation on land has not been much different; it's simply not as progressed owing to the inconstancy and periodically extreme harshness of the terrestrial environment. After millions of years of competition among hominids and apes only the extremely divergent forms survive, and the chimp and gorilla are doing quite poorly with all blame going to the human. They managed to survive by adopting lifestyles that reduced overlap of resources and environments with us and our ancestors.

To win on land meant killing the largest packages of meat and doing whatever facilitated that, including cooperation, language, weaponry and the intense study of animal behavior, the evolutionary origin of our interest in things whale. The key to human evolution and dominance was *winning* against some very tough customers: the lion and hyena in groups and larger in size than today's species; the bears, there's always the bears for northern or mountainous peoples, and bears are not only large, powerful and dangerous, they are quite intelligent; after the lions and bears were the wolves, also larger than the living varieties, and they hunted by day and in groups, like humans, and overlapped much with hominid niches, which is why we now have a dog. If you can't lick them, join them, the adage goes. In the face of extreme competition as must have occurred between wolves and hominids; one species is going to lose out over the long-run, and the wolf did; however, one branch of the wolf has much expanded its niche to include human dominated environments. The domestic dog was the interspecies communicator who came over from the other side, that side being the wolves we've beaten back to near extinction with much help from the wolf-turned-dog. Interspecies cooperation has proven to be immensely successful for dogs who were wolves and the humans who cooperated with them to hunt and make war against other predators and later, other humans. It's just possible that it was the dog-man connection that gave humans full dominance over such awesome beasts as lions, bears, wolves, hyenas, tigers and more. Which is one reason that we need take seriously the possible benefits from inter-species cooperation with dolphins, not merely for fishing or protection against common predators such as sharks, but for the next evolutionary stage of a dominant—self-rule—human-ity's most pressing need.

Competition between predators sharing an environment may best be described as violent warfare, the oldest the planet has known. This is the greatest lesson from evolution for us today: we arrived here by violent warfare, and that because somebody's been winning wars, and the advantages that entails, for millions of years. These old ways won't work anymore. Our crisis is coming to grips with ourselves, our predatory carnivo-rous/trophy hunting history. Because most of us are removed from interacting with predators, other than the civilized cat and dog, we must be reminded of the natural order of affairs in human life for most of our evolutionary past. Otherwise we shall miss the really poignant reason why delphinids and toothed whales are so important to us and our ability to usher in a new age of harmony.

Our perception of predators is quite paradoxical: we hate them and we love them. On one hand they are our most com-mon and beloved symbols, while on the other we hate and fear them so much that we kill them solely for the principle of the thing—the deeply rooted attitude that it pays off to kill your enemies if doing so doesn't cost too much. If we had not been predators ourselves, neither of these extreme attitudes would now exist; rather, we would simply fear predators for good rea-son. To understand all this, one needs to see a lion stare at a spotted hyena as though it despises it, and attack and kill hyenas but not eat them (when there is no food to contest or vulnerable kin present). Lions kill hyenas to kill them, period; this is not predatory behavior, not hunting, but hate between species. The same hate that the Japanese fishermen exhibit to dolphins they perceive as competitors for fish.

I studied the aggressive behavior of lions for many years, also that of tigers, other large cats and carnivores, and I learned that these creatures behave quite different when attacking their prey. Killed for food, the zebra hears no snarls from a lion that is choking it, nor does it see facial expressions associated with fighting between lions. But the hyena or leopard's view isn't a zebra's, precisely because the lion looks at a hyena the same way he does a male lion he hates and would fight to the death. Lions really hate hyenas, which is why they kill them, but both phenomena occur for one reason—it's in the lion's interest to kill his enemy if there isn't much risk (such as too many hyenas in one group, in which case the lion may be bested). A single lion may kill as many as three hyenas in seconds if it's got nothing better to do, and considering the risks that hyenas present to lions—predation on young, removal of potential lion prey and theft of lion kills—we shouldn't be surprised.

One may not become what Lilly calls a meta-programmer until one is succinctly aware of the existing programming that comes to us via natural selection and evolution. Neither may one come to appreciate what links us, both proximally and ultimately, to the predatory whales, and how they are alike and different than us. We humans were out there among the lions and hyenas and wolves for millions of years, and though we finally did dominate them, frankly, it was our relationships with them that made us what we are today: predatory, social, polygynous, large-brained, and highly sexual, like the toothed whales.

We owe the most of what we are to what were our greatest enemies, and that's exactly what Leopold implied when he said humility is required in the preservation of predators. He learned the hard way when he killed a she wolf and saw in her dying, green eyes something more eternal than trigger itch, and in that love/hate relationship, the wolf, lion, bear, eagle and orca symbolize more than conquest, trophy or dominion; they symbolize brotherhood. We coveted their position of power and eventually usurped their godhead. Man's most prevalent religious symbols are big cats, bears, raptorial birds and orcas, predators all, because these he emulated and imitated, and except for the orca, deceived, tricked, killed, stole from, and wiped out to become the undisputed master of his ship. Its the destiny of his soul that now is at issue.

The Ideal Predator-Prey System

PERHAPS THE LONG-TIME, DOMINANT predators of the sea, which may have evolved from early carnivores, are mellow compared to us by virtue of the fact that they have already resolved interspecies competition among themselves. The least we suspect is that their niches have been more finely tuned over greater time in a more stable environment. Perhaps their world is far more organized (except for the multitude of recent intrusions by humanity). There is one remarkable story from an Eskimo whaler who observed a pod of blue whales being followed by a group of orcas down the coast. The way in which the orcas came to eat a blue whale is of singular importance: not by chasing them, which orcas can do, then killing them with impressive coordination, but apparently by communicating with them underwater. In the Eskimo's words,

"The blue whales knew the killer whales were behind them and they went on for a while, and had this conversation between them. The one big old blue whale turned back out of the pack and he went back into the killer whales. They decided among them who was to be eaten."

Exactly how the blue whales decided who would go back to the orcas to be eaten, or whether the orcas asked the blues in some way to decide for themselves, we cannot know. What we may say is that here is efficient predation, an indication of the ideal predator-prey system, possibly the infusion of self-government in an orca-eat-blue-whale world, in short, cooperative predation. "Send us your hungry, your poor, your...*choice*?"

Do the dimensions of communication among cetaceans extend as far as predator communicating with prey? Perhaps behind what appears to be ruthless is a conscious balancing of life, deliberate, respectful giving and receiving? Whatever, this and countless observations throughout time and from around the globe indicate that we are dealing with a highly evolved, intricately adjusting community of beings in the sea. Their problem is man's attitude toward predators (competitors) and the earth at large.

Big Game Hunters

MALES ARE THE PREDATORS AMONG HUMANS. Both sexes are predatory among the toothed whales; however, what sets the human and orca apart from other cetaceans and primates is that both kill large, potentially dangerous species by cooperative behavior. The sperm whale specializes on giant squid, for which group hunting may be no advantage, and though the smaller dolphins definitely cooperate in hunting, they do not attack large, dangerous prey such as other cetaceans. They do cooperate in defense against predators such as sharks. Thus, in terms of fundamental niches, the human and orca are similar: both are "big game" hunters, a common trait that has much to do with their evolution of dominance.

Consider, for example, the possible role of learning, simulation, communication and teaching in orca societies compared to those of other toothed whales. In the orca's group attack, there is a premium on division of labor (roles), without which the attack could fail, not to mention that very large whales must be dangerous to predatory orcas. Humans not only hunted cooperatively for big game, they also confronted dangerous predators. Though now dominant, the human is well adapted to both orca-like hunting and dolphin-like defense against predators. In summary, humans converge with the high-ranking social predators among whales, and the same reasons that explain human social behavior, language and "intelligence" apply to the human-like whales.

Just as one may envision the origin of human language by *onomatapeia,* the imitation of animal sounds to attract or repel animals, then to communicate about them, delphinids may have developed a language system that depends upon the sonar echo from animals they hunt and kill.

Naturally, the imitativeness of human hunting would mean that hunters are apt to refer to a prey species or a predator in "terms" resembling the sounds made by or associated with these animals. Marine predators that use sonar to monitor the location, movement or condition of prey or enemies would be expected to refer to a particular animal according to its unique echo pattern, and "nouns" might be abbreviated representations of echoes—sound holograms. The closest thing in human life to a language built on sonar would be the use of sound-producing canes for blind people...the echoes vary predictably according to the nature of the object reflecting the sound, which the blind learn to discriminate. *If* one blind person could imitate the object-specific echo, he could transmit that sound to another person adept at reading echoes, and they would be en route to establishing a sonar-based language system.

How "Nice" are Dolphins and Orcas?

RELYING TOO MUCH ON BRAINS, too little on behavior, may have cost Lilly some acceptance of his ideas. He says that his studies, "of the brain of the dolphins gave us a faith that these were a sentient, compassionate, considerate species." *No* brain, not at present knowledge of them, could possibly indicate compassion or considerateness. Where, precisely, in any brain are these "functions" localized? And if complexity of brains were an indicator, then why is it that humans are bent on destroying whales, dolphins and one another? One could argue just the opposite: that increased cortical development indicates aggressiveness, warfare, and lack of compassion. That dolphins are, at least to certain species under particular circumstances, compassionate and considerate is so, but it is their *behavior* we refer to, not their brains. Despite everything Lilly would like to believe, not even the dolphins conform with the classical Roman Christian conception of "universal benevolence." Dolphins, like humans and lions, can be extremely compassionate *and* extremely uncompassionate. Dolphins are known to kill males of other delphinid species that were courted by a female in captivity. From the point of view of a Mahi Mahi, the dolphin-fish, dolphins would not seem overly compassionate. That neither dolphins or orcas make war, however, is highly significant, but neurological investigation would never indicate this to anyone. More serious, it is not at all clear that the brain is more than an organ in service of the mind, an ancient view which is being resurrected, in part, oddly enough, by neurophysiological research and Nobel laureates in that field.

Lilly confronts the modern misuse of the concept of anthropomorphism, an independently derived parallel in our thought. But, he tends to impute unwarranted human values to cetaceans so as to give a better image of them to humans. In the long run this not only discredits Lilly it also builds a false image of cetaceans, which could disserve them. He says, as example, that orcas eat "large fish and seals and some old dolphins...[and] parts of baleen whales that have been killed by man." That Lilly could twist an abundance of evidence around to present this "orcas are nice to whales" image is preposterous though others have done the same thing, knowingly or not, under the belief that other humans would like orcas more by thinking they "just eat fish." Neo-Marxist anthropologists have been guilty of the same thing when discussing human evolution and downplaying the radical importance of killing big game. We won't understand ourselves by pretending to be something we're not, or haven't been anyway, and neither will we comprehend the orca by egalitarianizing its image to conform with our own fantastic projections about what it means to be nice. Man's greatest danger to himself and the planet is his ability to deceive himself about his nature and intentions.

Orcas kill young and prime dolphins, not merely the aged, and they kill young and healthy, adult baleen whales, as well as belugas, walruses, sea lions, dogs, what have you except humans. Whalers named the orca "whale killer," mistranslated into English as "killer whale," for one reason only, that they killed whales. The same applies to Eskimos and coastal Indian whalers who widely and firmly recognize the orca's adeptness as a predator of great whales. The Latin term orca means "sea monster," and all these independently originating images are consistent: orcas kill whales, and their fundamental niche is that of "whale killer"...transients anyway.

If for many decades now the orcas have been killing fewer whales than their image seems to warrant then we should consider the tremendous decline in populations of prey owing to human whaling around the world. Some estimates place the great whale population at less than five percent of what it was three-hundred years ago. Whether we look to ethnographic evidence from sea peoples, especially whalers, European whaling logs, scientists' observations of orcas attacking whales or the orca's anatomy and social behavior, there is but one conclusion, that it is fundamentally adapted to kill other whales. As a social predator on large prey, like the wolf, lion or human, the orca is also well adapted to prey upon smaller organisms, perhaps now a necessity owing to a paucity of large whales. The wolves that kill moose during winter turn to mice and beaver during summer, and the lions that kill giraffe and buffalo during one season may rely upon gazelles and small antelope in other seasons, but for each of these species *what sets them apart from closely related predators is their capability to kill extremely large prey.*

A new view of the orca has emerged recently: there may be two races or species; a larger, coastal orca that preys upon fish primarily, and a smaller, transient variety that specializes on marine mammals. The Russians killed several hundred whales in the Antarctic, and examined their stomach contents, which resulted in these correlations. It is true that the coastal orcas studied for almost two decades in northern British Columbia and in Puget Sound prey mostly on salmon, though they could easily feed on seals, sea lions and cetaceans. So-called transient orcas moving through the fish-eating orcas' ranges have been seen to kill marine mammals— they represent individuals of a mammal-eating race. According to the study of a British scientist, the resident and transient races have not interbred for 100,000 years. We may have here a Cain and Abel story.

It is also popular among some cetologists and whale lovers to imagine that the orca rarely kills other whales, as though it wouldn't dare kill its "own kind." It has proved impossible in my experience to convince such believers otherwise. Lilly confounds the issue when he equates predation by orcas on *other* species of dolphins and whales as *murder*. Not only is the concept of murder a strictly human thing, it refers to killing members of one species, normally one's social group, and it is quite distinct from predation. To apply Lilly's thinking across the board, then lions that kill cheetahs and eat them are murderers, as are the West Africans who prey upon chimpanzees. In short, every predatory species that preys upon members of its family or order, which must be almost of them, are not predators but murderers, the worst abuse of anthropomorphism I can imagine.

Kindred Spirits?

WHALING LOGS ARE A SOURCE of information for understanding cetacean ecology and behavior. Lilly reviewed these for accounts of contacts between humans and orcas. Men thrown into the water with orcas which were feeding on dying whales were never injured or eaten. From this and similar data, Lilly concludes that the orca and other dolphins, which are also capable of killing humans, abstain from doing so because they know how dangerous humans are. I came to this same conclusion independently. However, one need be aware that some sea peoples may in fact *not* be potentially dangerous or retaliatory to delphinids, which is why further ethnographic work is important. One cannot abandon the possibility that delphinids look kindly upon us, not because it will benefit them, but because they perceive us as *spiritually* kindred to themselves, i.e., as capable of recognizing them as counterparts to us in the sea, a sort of mutual admiration society. As for the support of this idea, it is our own perception of cetaceans as intelligent, caring, aware and interesting beings which underscores our evolving relationship of reciprocity with them, and from all the evidence, their awareness of and interest in us predates ours in them.

The "kindred spirit" hypothesis for friendly, non-aggressive relationship between toothed whales and humans is not incompatible with the notion developed by Lilly and myself that they know better than to harm us because we would harm them even more. Either case would say a lot about the mentality of delphinids as being comparable to our own. The helping of humans without immediate reward, the avoidance of self-defense against humans by delphinids, and the lack of predation on humans by the orca, which otherwise attacks or plays with virtually every other mammal, marine or terrestrial, which frequents the sea or its shore, imply that the adage, "If you can't lick (eat?) them, join them," is as true for cetaceans as it is for humans. Such sophisticated assessments by delphinids regarding humans could be unique among wild animals, and the fact that, were we humans in their "shoes," confronted with a dangerous, inconquerable dominant, we would behave likewise means that delphinid and human mentality are comparable.

Sexual Behavior

LILLY *ASSUMES* THAT THE FREQUENT sexual behavior of cetaceans is play. The sexual behavior of delphinids especially is so persistent and common that its occurrence in virtually every context humans have observed suggests other functions than sexual play. Dolphins may employ sexual gesturing as a form of meta-communication, that is establishing a context for subsequent interaction, rather like an open-hand greeting functions in human life: "I come as a friend/not an enemy." Much of the dolphins' sexual gesturing appears to be a form of socializing. Males may rub erect penises against other males, females or juveniles, and the associated behavioral interactions indicate that such gesturing may communicate several things, for instance, friendship, courtship, dominance (of adult males) and so on. The same could be said of humans who are known to display erections under various contexts: aggressive warfare; communication of maleness and confidence, possibly intimidating to the enemy; social dominance, as of a stranger or new group member, in which case, homosexual contact may occur; and, the context of courtship and mating.

Lilly is not only ignorant of theories about the evolution of sexual behavior, he is ignorant of the *facts* of dolphin sexuality. Contrary to his assertion, dolphins are highly sexual not only in captivity but also in nature, so his explanation for frequent "sexual play" being a result of boredom does not hold up. *Why* a very few species of animals are extremely sexual, and these include the delphinids, big cats and the human, is another matter altogether, but the interested reader may refer to my article, Why some felids [cats] copulate so much: a model [theory] for the evolution of copulation frequency, which appeared in *Carnivore* I (1) 1978.

What Whales Learn

WE OFTEN SAY THAT JOHNNY *learned* to walk, but by that we do not really mean to say that he learned to walk in the same sense that we say Marvin learned to drive a car. A certain amount of experience is required for Johnny to walk, but the coordination for walking is *not* learned on the basis of experience, it is inherited. What Johnny is doing is practicing and perfecting an innately acquired pattern of movement specific to his human species. Anyone who doubts what I say must pause to give thought to how Johnny "learned" to crawl? Who, exactly, in Johnny's environment crawled? And if walking were strictly a matter of imitation of adults, then why is it that at the same ages, blind and even more severely handicapped children begin to pull themselves up and take steps? No evolutionist would expect walking or any other behavior so fundamental to human life to be primarily under the influence of learning per se.

By the same token, who would expect that any infant mammal has to *learn* to suckle? Lilly does. Ethologists have shattered such notions, outgrowths of Anglo-American empirical philosophy and behavioristic psychology. Infant humans are born quite well equipped to suckle a woman's nipple; moreover, actual learning of this complex behavior involving dozens of muscles and nerves, orientation and recognition of specific stimuli could only be "shaped" by long, tedious operant conditioning procedures in which case infants would starve before mastering the task. The experimental evidence supports what one would predict, and that is that natural selection would favor the evolution of innate patterns of behavior specifically adapted to assure that infants are able to feed from a woman's breast shortly after birth. Babies do learn all sorts of things, of course, though what they learn is largely governed by genetic blueprints. To answer Lilly's statement about baby dolphin's suckling behavior, it must be every bit as innate in origin as the mother's nipple.

Of course, dolphins do learn a tremendous amount, and Lilly gives examples of what appear to be teaching and cultural behavior. Though the young dolphin surely does not *learn* to bite and taste fish, as Lilly says, parents may present fish to infants as a means of teaching them which species are palatable as opposed to dangerous or poisonous. Cats, coyotes and gorillas similarly teach their young, and culture is a surprisingly ubiquitous phenomenon in non-human animals despite what cultural anthropology supposes. What kinds of information would be transmitted culturally among toothed whales?

Mountain sheep follow older individuals who know the way from experience to wintering grounds, some of which may not be visited for years until the severity of a winter demands it. Trophy hunting that selectively kills off those individuals who know the route and location of special wintering grounds may lead to entire herds dying out. The point is that, given the longer-term natural history of mountain sheep, one would not predict that wintering grounds are known through genetic or phylogenetically acquired information. The access to such grounds may change, as could the quality of forage, not to mention short-term climatic changes in alpine environments. No, the only efficient or effective means of sheep handling the uncertainty of good wintering range is experience itself, which, stored as memory, may be communicated, in this instance apparently by higher-ranking, older sheep who lead the way. Implicit in "leading the way" is to follow the leader. This is culture, nothing else.

As a linguistic creature, one that is *adapted* to use language in vitally significant ways, we would not expect language itself to be inherited, but we certainly would anticipate that humans inherit not only the anatomical/neurophysiological "machinery" essential to language use and acquisition, but also the underlying blueprint or structural pattern for language—what we mean by grammar. One might also expect a sensitive, maturational period for development of language skills, which, again, necessitates phylogentic meta-program-ming. All of which has been verified.

That we wouldn't expect the language to be the same for all human societies is reasonable: a) Different societies face funda-mentally different kinds of problems and in different ways, and as for the origin of language, such as by onomatapaeia, the variance in the things to be named and what they do or repre-sent will vary from environment to environment. Language is probably susceptible to the same stochastic processes as nature and the mind, so the randomness of historical events and the selection exerted by humans upon such randomness will mean variance of language even in the same environments so long as societies are relatively closed units; b) Different societies may benefit by "character displacement" in language. Two races of the same species of frog sound more different where their pop-ulations overlap than where they do not. The explanation from evolutionary behaviorism is that selection would favor diver-gence of mating calls in the overlap zone because this would help individual frogs mate with the right race.

Character displacement could also operate between human societies because of the advantages of hiding valuable informa-tion from individuals in other societies. As long as the reproductive interests of individuals correlates with their affilia-tion within a society, normally by kinship, then there will always be an advantage to hide certain information from mem-bers of other groups. The benefit of secreting information will continually push divergence of language, leading to dialects among societies with a common linguistic origin, and wholly different language systems ultimately. This is but one of many selective pressures on the divergence of language, and another reason that, beyond grammar, language is seemingly open-ended.

We know that many cetaceans, the toothed whales includ-ed, cover extremely large oceanic ranges, some species migrating over thousands of miles yearly. We know enough of marine ecology to say that for many of the toothed whales, whether residential or nomadic, resources are far from evenly distributed. Rather, they tend to be clumped, if not in space then in time, and so species like the orca and dolphin must be adapted to the same uncertainty of resources that human hunters were. On the one hand, certain locales often produce much food, at least at certain times of the year, while, on the other, these are not absolutely predictable. By the same token, there will be new sources of desirable food appear unexpectedly where they were not before or at an unusual time. Even the relatively stable marine environment undergoes radical shifts which could dramatically alter food species and their occurrence and predictability.

It seems irrefutable that dolphins employ vocal communication while actually hunting. They appear to give one another signals not only about the movement and nature of a food item, say, "Mahi mahi moving in your direction," but also use communication to coordinate one another's behavior so as to be able to catch the prey, "You move in that direction while I chase it and Harry over there can intercept it." The experiments that indicate that one dolphin can communicate abstractly the solution to complex learning problems to another, the highly cooperative behavior of dolphins catching fish or attacking enemies, and their use of sound communication in these contexts, speak for what constitutes language, albeit possibly a language much more complex, efficient and highly evolved than the human's.

And if one dolphin may communicate problem solving information to a second dolphin, then we know without a doubt that they are capable of using vocal communication to teach one another and their young how to solve vital problems. Indeed, considering the broad, realized niche of many toothed whales like the dolphin or orca, which feed on extremely varied prey species under widely variable conditions, which exploit divergent habitats ranging from shorelines to rivers to reefs and deep sea, and which continually adjust their survival strategies over huge ranges, teaching and culture would be very adaptive for them.

For language or its counterpart to operate in cetacean societies, individuals would need to be able to identify themselves and their group from other groups. Each dolphin has a signature whistle unique to itself expressed at the end of a sonic broadcast, and researchers can also identify dialects for each group of dolphins. Among orcas, it has been discovered that they also have individual signatures and group dialects. Scientists from the University of British Columbia and University of California at Santa Cruz have learned that the dialects of orcas of northern British Columbia resemble primitive human societies: each society has its own dialect, though three groups share the same dialect, and they are believed to be offshoots of one, original group. These three groups interact more often among themselves than they do with other groups, for example. But the most fascinating discovery has been that orcas *change* their dialect to match that of a foreign group they join temporarily...also not unlike humans.

More on Communication

IN CHAPTER SIX, LILLY DISCUSSES communication by sound in humans and cetaceans. Lilly summarizes his earlier, excellent observations on sound production by dolphins. Why he states that dolphins can't emit sounds in air for communication is peculiar since, clearly, they do, including in nature.

Moreover, there are reasons why one would expect them to, such as the advantage of avoiding detection by enemies underwater—the orca. Lilly's presentation of research that documents the ability of dolphins to match human sounds is thorough and convincing; the earlier work on which his review is based would seem sufficient to have received enthusiastic response from the scientific community.

In Chapter Seven, Lilly looks at nonverbal communication in apes, and he considers the limited vocal capacity of apes to be obscure to reason. Again, Lilly seems disinclined to employ "selective thinking" when it would be appropriate: the hypotheses about language evolution in humans normally rest upon comparisons between ancestral hominids and great apes and the selective pressures that would favor language in the former. Hunting, for instance, may have depended quite early on weaponry, which would mean that the hands and their communicative use would be limited, thus favoring vocal communication. And, to use vocal communication more effectively is to use it more often, but a species cannot afford to make a lot of sound which could attract dangerous predators unless it were higher ranking than the living great apes, and that must have been possible for hominids by virtue of weaponry, cooperative tactics and group size. Language may be beneficial over other forms of communication in some environments, for example, savannas or woodland edges, but risky due to frightening prey or attracting predators in denser habitats such as forests, where the apes live now and into which they may have been forced by hominid competition. Assuming what nearly everyone reckons to have been the case, the immense value of being able to communicate via sound under conditions in which scavenging or hunting were important and hominids faced an impressive array of formidable predators would have favored the evolution of linguistic capacities. These same selection pressures do not exist for the great apes, and it is not at all certain that their survival and reproductive success would be upgraded were they to be using vocal language. Vocally and gesturally they seem capable of achieving communication of information that humans might communicate linguistically, so one may doubt if in fact language in and of itself does more than communication by other means; however, within the context of the hominid niche of scavenging/hunting and defense against awesome predators, the chimpanzee's communication system would compare poorly to human language. It's not that language is absolutely better; I doubt for many reasons that it is, but certainly it was a highly adaptive thing for hominids living under their circumstances.

Lilly speculates that communicating with conspecifics by sound seems to be "beyond the ability of apes," and he assumes that brain size per se would be a necessary condition. This reasoning rather reminds me of the erroneous assumption made by comparative psychology for decades that intelligence in evolution and the animal world is structured according to some grand, Aristotelian chain of being, nothing less than a ladder, at top of which sits the great psychologist himself, of course. Lilly has been misguided for decades by assuming that there is a direct and *necessary* relationship between three variables: brain size, intelligence *and* language, as though language were the crowning glory of evolution.

Though Lilly employed Gregory Bateson's services, perhaps he did not learn Bateson's lessons very well, one of the most illuminating of which is that human language really is an inferior communication mode that does little if anything more than the so-called "affective" utterings of cats and dogs. Language is but a special case of communication, and neither may be expected to be adaptive for a lifeform unless they serve the survival or reproductive interests of individuals. I am saying that intelligence is not necessarily correlated with brain size, but rather must be defined or measured strictly according to the lifeform's existence within its natural environment, and, moreover, that language and communication evolve for the same reasons, not because of brain size or intelligence per se. That certain degrees of brain evolution may often be correlated with the occurrence of certain degrees of communication is a matter, again, of necessary but insufficient causation.

That chimpanzees have the brain size and "intelligence" to use sign language is obvious, despite the absurd criticisms that have been made. The fact that they don't use vocal language has nothing to do with their brain size or "intelligence," but with their history of evolutionary adaptation in different environments and niches than humans, as I said above.

If brain size were essential for phonal communication

between apes, as Lilly surmised, then it would be impossible to account for long-range sonic communication among wolves, lions, coyotes and so on. There are perfectly understandable evolutionary reasons why apes do not employ vocalizations as much as hand and other gestures and expressions to communicate. Lilly's presuppositions lead him to the wrong questions and the wrong answers. Despite his revolutionary interest in animal intelligence, he thinks like a nineteenth century man, seemingly oblivious to the radical meaning of behavior *and* anatomy as adaptations to environments.

15

Communicating
with Dolphins

DOLPHINS HAVE BEEN BEFRIENDING people for millennia. There are accounts of it in all the classical literatures of the world, and prehistoric art from Europe to South Africa suggests that our ancestors delighted as much in swimming with dolphins then as we do now.

In this century, numerous dolphins have befriended people. Pelorus Jack in New Zealand daily guided the ferry back and forth between the islands for years. Beaky, a bottle-nose dolphin otherwise known as Donald and Horace, towed boats in Falmouth Harbor, southern England, where he also towed children who held onto his dorsal fin. Beaky also abducted two women while they were swimming and attempted to make love to them. They described his behavior as sensual and harmless.

While Nicola and her pod initiated a meeting of nations with us in British Columbia, the most remarkable friendship has been established between people and dolphins at Monkey Mia Beach, northwest Australia. For twenty years, the dolphins have been arriving twice daily to offer people on the beach live fish. Apparently, a fisherman gave a female dolphin a live fish. The next day she arrived at the shore with a live fish in her mouth, and offered it to a person. Over time the number of dolphins bearing gifts of live fish to people has increased steadily to over 15.

Human cultures that do not share languages establish friendships by exchanging gifts, which clearly communicates their intentions. It seems that the dolphins of Monkey Mia are doing the same.

The only people-friendly dolphins in the western hemisphere at this time are around Hilton Head Island, South Carolina. These bottle-nose dolphins commonly approach boats and solicit petting from people.

More surprising they accept dead fish as food. Normally dolphins in captivity refuse dead fish for weeks, but there is no reason to suspect that this pattern at Hilton Head may have started with an escapee. Apparently, it began in 1976 when a commercial fisherman began to give fish from his catch to a friendly bottle-nose.

Helping people catch fish is a clear communication of friendship. Dolphins annually show up at an island off North Africa where they systematically drive fish into the natives' nets. The help of the dolphins supplies enough fish to feed the people of the island for another year. Daily off the coast of Brazil, friendly dolphins help local fisherman catch fish. There are similar accounts from the South Pacific where islanders hit rocks together underwater to signal to the dolphins, which come to drive fish into their nets. Interspecies communication between dolphins and humans is ancient and takes many forms.

Meta-Communication

LANGUAGE IS BUT A SMALL SEGMENT of a huge spectrum of communicative behavior and techniques. Dogs respond to human speech, but they often communicate with us in the form of gestures which are meta-communicative. When your dog stamps its paws on the ground while lowering its front end then turning and running to the side it is inviting you to play. Imitating this behavior, humans may invite dogs to play. The communication is about communication, "Let's interact now in a playful way.,"

There are more than a few men and women whose lives changed dramatically owing to their meta-communications with dolphins and orcas, largest member of the dolphin family. One is Dr. Paul Spong. Like me, he was a university professor in animal behavior. Like me, Spong went to see orcas in captivity, and when he saw them and interacted with them, he left the university and set out to study them closely. So did I. It all began for Spong when an orca taught him a lesson.

Spong had been sitting at the edge of the Vancouver Aquarium pool with his shoes and socks off, his feet dangling in the water. When the female Skana came up next to him, he instinctively withdrew his feet from fear Skana might bite him. She did. As Spong jerked his feet away, Skana quickly raked her teeth over his feet. Again, Skana surprised Spong, again he jerked and again she raked her teeth over his skin.

Spong tried to overcome his fear, but it was not until after ten trials in which he jerked his feet away and Skana harmlessly raked them that he succeeded in leaving his feet in the water. And as soon as he did that Skana stopped raking his feet. According to Spong, Skana taught him to overcome his fear. He had nothing to fear all along. If Skana had wanted to harm Spong she would have bitten his feet off the first time. Skana was only presenting opportunities over and over until Spong was able to make it to Step-2 or duetero learning. Gregory Bateson calls it meta-learning. Something dolphins and orcas master in about the same number of trials required by Spong. In fact, dolphins and humans rate equally in several kinds of learning experiments.

When Gregory Bateson was working with John Lilly in the Bahamas, he and a colleague tried a little experiment. Bateson's friend wondered if the female dolphin would save him if he acted like he were drowning. He swam out where it was deep then went through his fake drowning maneuvers. The dolphin came to him immediately and took him to shore. Then the man had a truly brilliant idea. He wondered if she'd save him a second time. He repeated the performance, but in Bateson's words, she beat him up. Dolphins are expert at administering a trouncing without causing serious injury.

Rescuing a human can't be explained with simple notions about dolphin adaptations or instinctive tendencies. If dolphins rescue people because of some blind instinct, then why didn't she rescue the man again? Beating the man up is a meta-communication, "Don't pretend to be drowning when you're not." Whack! She fathomed the game and scolded the man severely for making light of what should be better taken seriously by dolphins, by humans, and by humans needing dolphins. No perspective offers any indication but that the dolphin accurately assessed the situation, communicated that quite obviously to the experimenter, and in her communication not only told the man he shouldn't do that, she also said something about the values that dolphins uphold about life. My guess is that any mature female dolphin would severely scold an adolescent dolphin stupid enough to fake drowning. Drowning is no joke to a dolphin. But these creatures are well known for their playfulness and humor, another indicator of their advanced intelligence.

The funniest communication between humans and delphinds was related to me by Dr. Simon Cotton, first man to film wild orcas and humans swimming together. A physician who fell in love with orcas, Cotton took his professional film crew out to swim with the whales. The orcas accommodated Cotton and the crew, to the point of standing on their heads, upside down in the water. Four adult males lined up side by side with their bellies facing the camera, each of them with an erection. Cotton thinks that the orcas knew they were on camera and behaved appropriately under the circumstances. As a matter of record, no one else around the world after twenty years of intense behavioral study has recorded them standing on their heads in synchrony sporting erections.

Exactly how orcas may perceive what we would perceive on film as sophisticated humor is a mystery, but then that's why I keep wondering if they know us better than we know ourselves.

Wade Doak sent me pictures of his wife, Jan, swimming with dolphins in an imitation dolphin suit. When Jan entered the water with the dolphins she propelled herself with pectoral fins held in her hands close to her body and by kicking with both feet simultaneously. Her legs were held together in a dive suit with only one leg. A single fin held both of her feet. On her back was strapped a dorsal fin.

As soon as the dolphins observed Jan they began to instruct her in how to swim like a dolphin. One of the dolphins placed its body immediately in front of her and broadside while it very slowly demonstrated dolphin swimming motions. Especially important was the dolphin's use of a single fluke for propulsion. The dolphins watched Jan closely until she was able to move both legs as one member of her body. They corrected her as she practised until, she claimed, it was possible for her to swim tirelessly under water for hours.

As soon as the dolphins observed Jan in the dolphin suit they seem to have recognized her meta-communication: I want to be like you. The mechanistic minded scientist might propose that the dolphins actually perceived Jan as a dolphin, a rather inept one, and that is why they set out to teach her to swim like one. We know that dolphin sonar penetrates bodies; a sonar scan of Jan would indicate she is other than dolphin. We also know that their visual acuity is comparable to our own, in which case it would have been obvious that Jan was not a dolphin. Furthermore, dolphins do not teach one another how to swim. If that were the case, most dolphins would drown within a few minutes after birth. They are born able to swim, with the proper coordinations fully intact.

Clearly, the dolphins perceived Jan as a human who wanted to play dolphin with them. They read her imitative appearance as a meta-communication: I would like to interact with you. The Doaks followed the right course, penetrating because it was simple-minded, innocent and childlike.

An Encounter of the Third Kind?

NEARLY 25 YEARS AGO in northern British Columbia, Erich Hoyt conducted an experiment that conforms with the book and film, *Encounters of the Third Kind*. His experiment consisted of broadcasting underwater an imitation of the greeting call of the orca. With a synthesizer, Hoyt did his best to produce an imitation, but even to his ear the imitation greeting call was decidedly not the same as the orca's. Moreover, he was able to imitate only the lower end of the orca's call, a frequency band ranging up to perhaps 25,000 cycles per second, compared to the orca's upper range of 250,000 cycles per second.

The point is simply this: there is no reason to believe that orcas would perceive Hoyt's synthesized greeting call as emanating form another orca. That is precisely why his results are so startling. As soon as he broadcast the imitation, the orcas immediately responded. Not with their greeting call, *but with a precise imitation of his imitation.* And that incredible event not only conforms with the fictional plot of humans encountering ETs, it confirms the prediction of the world's foremost space scientists as to what we might expect extra-terrestrial intelligent life to do in response to our radio signals. Now you know why people like myself have turned our attention to the inner space of the sea to encounter intelligent life.

When I wrote a letter to *Science*, among the most prestigious of scientific journals, regarding Hoyt's experiment and its significance, it was returned without comment.

'Tephui': Breaking the Code?

WADE DOAK WAS OUT in his sailing vessel looking for wild dolphins in the waters around New Zealand. He had one of the country's largest TV stations' field crew aboard to film some of the dolphins Wade and his wife Jan had encountered one year earlier. The name of their boat was Project Interlock, the symbol a Yin/Yang, and inside the Tao emblem a mermaid encountering a dolphin. The mermaid in the human/dolphin interlock was fashioned after Jan wearing a one-legged wet suit to imitate the conformation of the dolphin's body and fluke.

The TV crew got lured into accompanying the Doaks out into the sea after Wade and an American psychic appeared on a TV show in New Zealand. The psychic had a dream in which a dolphin spoke to him and said "Tephui." The dream was aboard Doak's boat, and when the psychic awoke he asked Wade what the word tephui meant. Wade thought it could be a Maori word.

On the TV program with Wade and his psychic friend was the foremost wiseman of the Maoris, a man recognized by many Europeans and natives throughout the South Pacific as a genuine seer or prophet. They asked the sage what the word tephui meant in Maori, and recounted the psychic's dream. The old sage said that when a dolphin comes to a man in his dream that dream is not a dream but real. According to him, dreams of dolphins are actual communication with the dolphin on a higher plane. The same has been claimed independently by numerous psychics up and down the entire west coast of America, some of whom have reported a higher incidence of strandings within two weeks after they dream about whales.

The Maori sage also said that tephui is the Maori word for dolphin. It is the name they use to call the dolphin, to make it come and communicate with it.

Sure enough, one year to the day later in the same place, Wade's boat and guests encountered the same dolphins. The crew frolicked in the water with the friendly dolphins who swam around them again and again, making merry and playing with the humans. After a long filming session guided by everyone's shared celebration, Wade thought back on the word tephui and what the Maori wiseman had told him. He ran to the highest point on deck and yelled out loud, "Tephui! Tephui!"

As one organism, the several dozen dolphins grouped together for the first time and in perfect unison dolphin-leaped side by side over and over again around all the humans and their craft. Then they disappeared. Whatever tephui meant when yelled out by Wade Doak we may never know, but the response was unique in his experience, the only time he ever saw dolphins group up and move as they did in perfect synchrony, so many dolphins alongside one another, nor did he ever see them execute a circle leaping and diving together around his boat or anyone else's. The grammar of the entire interaction distinctly points to tephui as communicating something significant to the dolphins, and their behavior would certainly indicate some effort on their part to communicate something of significance to the humans. Perhaps their circular motion and unified ranks were meant to communicate oneness, i.e., that all of us are one in the great circle of life.

After Wade Doak had communicated to me the story I've recounted, I set to thinking about the word tephui. The name given in imitation of a creature's sounds, onomatopoeia, is how we got the words/names for the lion and wolf—the sounds of a lion roaring and a wolf wuffing. The Maoris were very much a sea-people, and they must have frequently contacted dolphins. They did not kill or eat dolphins, and consider them sacred, intelligent and helpful, as do most societies in the Pacific. If tephui is an ancient Maori word for dolphin then perhaps the Maori used onomatopoeia to invent the word; maybe tephui sounds like a dolphin. . . ?

Well, actually, it does. Take the first syllable, "t." Say "tee." Notice the strong blowing sound produced by holding the tongue against the roof of the mouth. Now, add the second letter and phonate "te," not as tee but as "ta." If you extend the phonic component so that the sound is uttered forcefully with emphasis on the t, you will make a sound resembling the exhalation or "blow" of a dolphin. Now, say "phui" like phooey and then say phooey by drawing your air inwards rather than expelling it. *That* is the sound the dolphin makes when it inhales, a phooey in reverse. And there is tephui. Te for exhaling, phui for inhaling, so naturally one might think that the Maoris called the dolphin by its name, the sound it makes. All dolphins who have interacted with Maoris through however long they have shared the sea have said one thing predictably, Te-phui.

I wrote this notion to Wade Doak, who wrote back to say he had come to the same hypothesis. What he and I also came up with independently was that the sound tephui may have still more meaning, not only to humans but to dolphins. If dolphins had a word for us, what would it be like? If not in straight delphinese then translated into hominese. Applying the same principle of onomatopoeia, the most familiar, predictable sound made by every human who shared the sea with dolphins would have been the sound of exhaling and inhaling in rapid succession. To appreciate the similarity of the word tephui to the sound of a person swimming, pretend you are swimming and listen to your imitation of that experience as you lift your head up to the side, let your breath out sharply and quickly, then listen to the sound of your inhale as your head is brought back into the water...te phui. The *universal* sound of humans in the sea is tephui.

Now, *if* delphinese were structured on onomatopoeia, then the dolphin word for human could be tephui or their version of that sound. That would mean that the Maori word for dolphin would be the same as the root form of the delphinese "word" for human. And to take it a step further, the dolphins may communicate tephui to humans who are psychically receptive to it as a way of communicating, "We know that you should call us te-phui, that by saying te-phui to you now, I inform you that I am aware of your name for me." Or, "The word that symbolizes us both, our common heritage, which is to breathe at the interface of sea and air, is the sound we both make there. . .our common denominator."

If dolphins are the creatures I believe they are, then, applying the exobiologist's assumptions to communication with them, I would look for the sound made by both humans and dolphins everywhere, reproduce that sound and communicate it to them and listen to their response. If any human being reported to me that in a dream or any other state a dolphin said te-phui to him, I would take that as support for my hypothesis that dolphins understand better how to establish communication with humans—meta-communication—than humans do with dolphins. And one might even expect that those individuals who are most receptive to psychic communication, which happen not to be the vast majority of scientists, but people we call psychics, would "hear" dolphins "say" tephui. Perhaps the Maoris intuitively comprehended everything I am trying to state in a linear, rational manner; whatever, the line of thought that a psychic's dream influenced may hold the key for decoding delphinese and communicating with dolphins.

16

Do Orcas and Dolphins Never Lie?

JOHN LILLY AND OTHERS have worked toward *linguistic* communication with dolphins. The results have been less than spectacular, resembling the early work with chimpanzees. Raised with human infants in a home setting, young chimps never managed to utter more than a few words. These studies suggested great frustration on the part of the chimps, who couldn't keep pace with the language maturation of their human sibs. Chimpanzees are not adapted to use speech. Only when the Gardners of Reno recognized that chimps may be able to use hand-language was a breakthrough made with the apes.

My guess is that the current interspecies communication research on dolphins is making the same kind of error as was made with the chimps. Dolphins do use sound to communicate, but it is doubtful that they use anything comparable to human speech, which is linear, with sound symbols spaced sequentially over time. It appears that dolphins are brilliant enough to figure out what is expected of them by Louis Hermann's research team in Hawaii. They are able to make fairly subtle distinctions about human requests (questions), and their responses suggest that they understand simple sentences. While dolphins and people aren't yet conducting sophisticated conversations, they certainly are communicating well.

Unlike the orca and dolphins, which have evolved in a water medium where sound is the most efficient mode of perception, we humans rely primarily on vision. Our perception relies upon the reflection of light from the surface of objects. Which means that deception is inevitable. A human may be frightened and lacking in confidence, but appear to be unafraid and confident. Probably all of us have practised the adjustment of our posture, facial expressions and tone of voice precisely to deceive others. In fact, much of human life is sheer deception.

The young man knocking on the door of a girl's home may be shaking in his boots from fear of rejection, but as he stands there he prepares himself to give the opposite appearance. He tries to stop his knees from shaking, takes a deep breath, pulls his shoulders back, wipes his sweating palms off, and mentally simulates a friendly relaxed smile and a steady, assured voice. If her father comes to the door, he had better give a firm handshake with a dry palm, and his voice better not quiver. He thinks to himself that he should look directly in the man's eyes, not glance sideways to indicate his insecurity. Once inside he should remember to keep his hands out of his pockets to appear relaxed. All to make a good first impression he will do his very best to deceive others.

The young man is not alone. The whole process of applying for a job involves projecting a confident and relaxed demeanor despite contrary emotions. In aggressive confrontations, men are master deceivers—they puff out their chests, inflate their lats, flex their thighs and adopt facial expressions and speech which deny their inner fear and impulse to run. On the other hand we often deceive others into believing we are unthreatening or submissive. When we feel angry, it may behoove us to make every effort to appear calm, strike a smile rather than a frown, and speak softly and slowly rather than yell out loud. When stared at by several unfamiliar males a man will do his best to seem docile by avoiding eye contact, stooping his shoulders, moving slowly and speaking in a low voice.

All around the world humans of extremely divergent cultures employ a wide range of facial expressions and postures to communicate efficiently on a non-verbal level. A German man recognizes flirtatious behavior in New Guinea, as well as an Ethiopian girl recognizes the frown of an Englishman. All of which suggests that our basic repertoire of expressions is universal, a product of evolution. While we learn to consciously manipulate our expressive behavior to deceive others, the ability to do so with great proficiency also indicates that natural selection has favored the evolution of our uncanny ability to deceive. It may have begun with hunting, in which hunters imitate and mimic their prey. Whistling, for example, surely began with the hunting of birds, and speech itself may have evolved from imitating the sounds made by an animal to attract or repel it, and to communicate about it to other hunters.

Deception is so common in the everyday life of people that it is surprising that we aren't more aware of it. How many times have we been asked, "How are you doing today?", and though we're feeling lousy or having a bad day, we respond, "Fine, just fine." A flat out lie. Often it is in our interest, meaning our success, to pretend to others that we are something we are not. We tell our parents that we did our homework when we didn't because that could mean use of the family car Friday night. We tell the boss that we are enjoying the job when in fact we detest it, but lying to him may mean a promotion or higher pay. The payoff for being a good liar has been immense for hundreds of thousands of years in many realms of human life, and it is no wonder that it has influenced the reproductive success of individuals and the perpetuation of genes conducive to lying.

To take it all one step further, perhaps evolution has favored *self*-deception. Robert L. Trivers postulated this most dramatic idea. He argued that if we really believe we are trustworthy, then we would be better able to convince others to cooperate with us in ways that benefit us (and our reproductive success). He takes as the special case our selfishness. If we can convince others that we are unselfish, then they should be more likely to cooperate with us. They may go ahead and help us now, as with food or protection, believing that at some later date we may reciprocate. Most humans are unable to admit they are selfish, when to merely exist demands selfishness. A truly unselfish being would not eat food that could be eaten by anyone else, for example. Usually, as we begin to recognize our selfishness, we become anxious, feel guilty and repress such thoughts or find ourselves insisting that we don't have to be selfish when clearly we do at least to some extent. Trivers believes that natural selection has favored the evolution of self-deception: we instinctively believe we are unselfish because this serves our self-interests!

Our problem in the world is our selfishness—it is what lies behind the over-exploitation of resources, the extermination of species including whales, and the possibility of global war. We can ill afford to continue pretending we are unselfish when in fact it is selfishness that threatens our very survival. Before we can honestly admit both the source of our success and of our present problems, we have to realize that self-deceptions have been adaptive. But our new adaptation must involve a major change in viewpoints, so that we see that competition severely threatens our self-interest, while cooperation between individuals and societies and species, represents the new adaptive selfishness. Today, to survive and have reproductive success, individuals will have to expand their self-interests to encompass more people, more things, and more of nature.

Now, what has all this to do with whales? Among the dominant predators of the world, including humans, the orca and dolphins have the most stable societies and they do not seem to make war, perhaps because they cannot lie to one another.

Perception by sonar may reveal motives and thus prevent the evolution or use of social deception. If this is so, what do these creatures know about themselves, about one another, about us? What might we learn to do and how might we change from understanding them?

While the orca and dolphins have visual acuity comparable to our own, their sonar exceeds anything we could imagine in the sensory realm. They use sonar the way we employ X-ray machines. An orca can literally see through another orca. Sonar penetrates bodies, which are the same density as seawater. Which means that the delphinids and other toothed whales cannot deceive one another. Two males vying for a female would not have to fight it out because each could accurately assess the others prowess.

We use lie detectors to discover what we cannot see with the eyes or hear with the ears. A human consciously may deceive us, but he cannot hide his internal responses. Imagine how very different our life would be if we were able to see beyond surface images of reflected light. We wouldn't deceive one another, and self-deception never could have evolved. Our communication would be wholly honest, and far more accurate. In fact our minds, our self-awareness and our societies would be quite different. Why fight with someone else if you already know ahead of time that he would best you? The apparently friendly stranger on the street would be detected as a thief or rapist. The politician's actual motives would be known. Con men wouldn't exist. A person incapable of performing a function likely wouldn't be given the task. Illness would be quickly and cheaply diagnosed. Quality of food items would be detectable, and the examples go on and on.

We have begun to utilize sonar in medicine, but it must be incredibly primitive compared to the sonar of toothed whales. An orca should be able to quickly examine another orca's muscle tone, and turgidity, blood pressure, heart rate, emotional status, size, and, perhaps indirectly, its thoughts. In humans there are precise correlations between various physiological parameters and emotions, and by monitoring muscle contractions during sleep it is even possible to predict the subject matter of a person's dreams, such as playing tennis. Impressive as such advances are they must be primitive by orcas' standards.

The absence of deception should minimize conflicts of interest among individuals—no lying, no cheating, no need to make lengthy evaluations of intentions or the suitability of mates, etc. Likewise, cooperation should be enhanced, exceedingly more efficient. These musings may point in part to why, for the ruler of the sea, serious combat is so extremely rare. Peace among men will come from peace within them, but if self-deception blinds us to the very nature of our problem is it possible to "know thyself"? I believe it is possible, but very difficult. All the problems of the world and its creations come down to healing our emotional wounds for only by that process of descent may we transcend the illusions and self-deceptions of ego. Here is the real work. Maybe inner peace is something the orca takes for granted.

The Most Advanced Communication System?

WHILE THE SQUEAKS AND WHISTLES made by dolphins and orcas when they communicate don't resemble their sonic emissions, aptly described as clicks, it is reasonable to suppose that a species that uses sonar to monitor its world would evolve a communication system derived from sonar. We know that dolphins can communicate complex information to one another with remarkable efficiency. In a now classic experiment in problem solving, the dolphin who solved the problem after several trials, communicated to the next dolphin, who was ignorant of the experiment, through a water channel connecting them. The second dolphin entered the experimental tank and immediately solved the problem. Dolphins and orcas are the most vocal species on earth, and their auditory brains are by far the most developed, indicative of the importance of communication by sound.

When toothed whales emit sonic beams, they receive echoes back from objects within the sonic beacon. The echoes are 3-dimensional because of the time differential involved in the penetration of bodies by sound. The best way to imagine what they perceive with sonar is to think of Superman with X-ray vision. He would see light reflected not merely from the surface but also from each layer of tissue underneath, all the way through a body. The information content received by an orca using sonar or Superman using X-ray vision would be many magnitudes greater than what we see from only surface reflections. It might take us hours using speech merely to describe everything we see in detail in a few seconds. That is the problem with human communication: we perceive the world with vision, but then attempt to communicate about it with speech. A mere moment of visual perception of surface reflections of light has to be translated into minutes or hours of expression by speech. In other words, our communication mode, speech, is linear—it takes time to describe what we have seen instantaneously, and if this weren't inefficient enough, the leap from one modality to another has been proven to be very inaccurate. In introductory psychology classes we used to flash a slide of the shooting of President Kennedy in front of all the students. No two verbal descriptions were ever the same, and all were grossly incomplete.

To appreciate what it means to use the same modality to perceive the world *and* communicate about it, as orcas and dolphins do, imagine for a moment that Superman has found a way around the problem of translating X-ray vision into speech. Suppose that he could also communicate with vision by transmitting light to your eye. You would receive in a single emission of light all that he has seen in X-ray. Now that would be a very advanced communication system. Not only does it provide X-ray information, as sonic echoes do, it *transmits* precisely what is received. If we could use vision as Superman does, and also communicate with it, our knowledge of the world would be quantum leaps beyond what it is, and our exchange of information would be light-years faster. A university education that now takes four years might require a few hours, and it would be a far better education.

Well, except for the fact that orcas and dolphins use sound instead of light this is basically the situation, I think, that exists for them. Of course, they would not communicate everything they perceive from sonic echoes, but rather abbreviated sound "pictures" which eliminate superfluous information. I believe they transmit sound holograms, which contain not only information about the environment, such as prey, but also their ideas. It seems likely to me that a brief sound emission transmitted from one orca to another contains more information than we could communicate in several minutes, but much more accurate.

From spending thousands of hours observing orcas while listening to their underwater communication, I suspect that in a single "flash" of sound one orca can effectively communicate to another that, "There is a densely packed school of 100 chum salmon straight ahead of you 50 yards which is diving fast. You dive below them to drive them towards the surface, and I'll intercept them and breach to stun them. You blast them (with sonar) from below to stun some (which you may eat) and drive the others to the surface, where I'll breach and stun some for myself and for my young son. Let's maintain silence until they surface. Now go."

The instantaneous communication by sound probably also includes critical environmental information, such as topography of the sea bottom, shoals or fishing nets, and refined data about the prey—degree of schooling, speed of movement, angle of descent, and so on. All the things we would detect with our eyes, and a lot more, but which we are unable to transmit with speech without taking so long that the effort would be wasted. Even our most sophisticated communication systems, as used in the military and satellite communication systems, pale when compared with what the orcas and dolphins must achieve.

Now just because orcas may not deceive one another is no reason to suspect they don't practise deception on other species. They do, all the time. While one dolphin chases a mahi mahi it appears to communicate to a member of its group where and how to intercept the fish. Orcas seem to lob their flukes against the surface to frighten schools of salmon towards other orcas that anticipate the fish and catch them unaware. And when transient orcas move through the waters of the local residents they often maintain complete silence, and seem to be trying to avoid detection by the locals. And there is abundant evidence to indicate that orcas are skilled at deceiving their captors, which is why they were so difficult to capture in Puget Sound. Though it may be difficult for one orca to deceive another as to its intentions or prowess, they are master deceivers of prey and enemies.

But the dolphin use of sound does not end here. Ken Norris of Santa Cruz, an imaginative natural historian discovered what we should have suspected from the reports of divers in the water with orcas. That dolphins use sound as a weapon. They can emit sonic blasts equivalent to a blasting cap going off under water at a distance of 50 yards or so. Which is how they stun fish and catch them easily. Ensonification, as Norris termed it, suggests all sorts of things—that dolphins could employ sound to make war on one another, and if not against their own kind, say members of competing groups, then against their enemies. Competition has been observed between dolphins, but none of it very serious; however, no one has been watching or listening for the use of sound as weaponry.

Interviewing divers for years, I heard several reports of men describing the feeling of orcas coming. They described being struck by sonar blasts prior to knowing there were orcas anywhere nearby. My guess is that the orcas were sending out sonic emissions for monitoring purposes, and detected the divers at a distance underwater. The typical report of this phenomenon stated that once the initial blasts were felt by the divers, they weren't repeated, and then the orcas either appeared close by or avoided the divers. There is a close correlation between the attitude of divers toward orcas and the orcas' interaction with them following detection. If the diver was afraid of orcas, the orcas inevitably went around him. If the divers were not afraid, such as men who have been involved in orca captures, the orcas often approached them closely, even touching them slightly while passing.

DAVE PORTER

Telepathy experiment in which the author mentally asked Skana to come to him.

17

Psychic Communication

REPORTS OF PSYCHIC COMMUNICATION with dolphins and orcas are legion. Many individuals who have participated in our volunteer studies of orcas and dolphins have reported them. They have become so commonplace in my personal experience that I no longer think about testing it experimentally. As an example, on our last day with the orcas in Puget Sound in the summer of 1991, we were taping video for a film production about orcas. The camera man was riding on the bow of the Yaki Taki, pointing his camera at me in an inflatable boat. I placed my boat on the other side of orcas from him, so he could get us and them in the picture. While we were cruising alongside the orcas I said outloud to them, "O.K., you guys. I've been working for you for years. A lot of children are going to see this film, so put on a show now."

Immediately a cow came up out of the water and spy-hopped at me, then she did a full breach right next to the boat, all of it on camera. Coincidence or communication? I can tell you that in 16 years no orcas had ever breached close to my boat. Something I take pride in, because I believe they often breach by boats to warn them to stay back. I have tried never to disturb or irritate them, though many tourists and researchers do, and that is how they get spectacular photos of breaching. That day was the only time I had ever asked the orcas to perform, and the only time they ever did.

We were along the east side of Orcas Island in 1994 when we came upon two pods of resident orcas. Most of the adults formed a circle about 150 feet in diameter. Then there was the most dramatic bout of breaching I'd ever witnessed. It looked like orca fireworks as one individual then another breached. Analyzing the video tape later, I counted almost 35 breaches in 30 seconds.

A few minutes after the show I ran my inflatable boat into the tender ship to pick up my wife Cathy. The water was rough but she wanted to come out with me to be close to the orcas. So far that summer she had been confined to the 50 foot long boat with our infant son, Drake.

Cathy is a holistic healer with awesome vital lifeforce and psycho-spiritual faculties. While we were motoring about a hundred yards away from a sub-group of orcas she asked them, silently in her mind, to show us love.

That they did. Surrounded by several young orcas who seemed to be keeping an eye on us by spyhopping a pair of adults began courting and mating. I was fascinated with the whole ritual as I had observed copulation a few times in many years, and never had it occurred with youngsters surrounding the mating pair. Only afterwards did Cathy tell me what she asked the orcas to do.

Though we don't know how orcas do it they often seem to know things about us, and they respond in ways that communicate that. The four bull orcas standing upside down with erections in front of the movie camera is a good example.

During the 1995 season a man named David joined an Orca Project expedition. His lifelong dream had been to swim with a wild orca whale. During his expedition we encountered and observed numerous orcas, but the conditions were never suitable for him to get in the water with them. As we had to relocate our campsite, and David was free for a few extra days, he stayed on to help us. After camp was moved he went out in one of our boats with Peter Carstens, our able assistant from Germany. They found orcas below Lime Kiln Point and moved south with them.

Two bull orcas swam close alongside their boat. At a distance of a few feet they rolled over on their backs and stuck their erect penises in the air, and cruised that way for several minutes. Then Dave got into the sea with the orcas. They blasted him sonically and he climbed back into the boat. His dream had come true, and he was a changed person.

What I did not mention was that David is a homosexual, the only one as far as we know who ever participated in the Orca Project. I say this because in almost twenty years of observation of wild orcas this incident was the only one in which orcas conspicuously displayed their penises. Mere coincidence? I doubt it. I am inclined to agree with Peter, qualified witness of the entire affair who interprets the behavior of the orcas to have been communication that they knew David is a homosexual.

In the summer of 1995, I learned much about how to communicate with orca whales. I had had numerous telepathic communications with them but something was missing. My guidance showed me that I needed to hold in my heart the intention and the image of communicating with the leaders of the orca pods. And send that intention and image out the top of my head through the pranic tube.

During the Orca Project '95 often I asked the leaders of the groups for the members to open the hearts of the people and to demonstrate their power, beauty and grace. Almost always the orcas immediately put on a lovely show. My confidence in the new technique was bolstered.

One group of volunteers had not seen an orca. Daily I had sat down and asked for guidance about where the orcas would be at what time so we could locate them. They were out on the Pacific side of Vancouver Island, beyond the reach of our small boats. On the group's last day we were motoring down the west side of San Juan Island toward Lime Kiln Point. Feeling a little desperate, I did not ask for guidance as to the location of orcas but instead asked for them to come to us. It was about 1:00 PM and I asked them to be there at Lime Kiln Point at 4:00 PM.

We went into the beach just south of Lime Kiln Point, and I got out the binoculars. I thought I saw something out in the Straits of Juan de Fuca, so I headed out that way by myself. The water was rough, but the further I went the more certain I was that the orcas were moving east from the Pacific.

As I approached the pod moving east I encountered a small group of six orcas heading northeast. I turned to follow them straight back to Lime Kiln Point, where they arrived at 3:57 PM. They did not fish along the way, and once they arrived at Lime Kiln they turned around to head south. We followed them as they swam back to the main pod, still heading east.

There is a difference between asking for guidance and asking for what we want. Ask and you will receive. That day was an important lesson for me. I had overlooked my own power.

18

Should We
Talk to Them?

I ENTERED "CETOLOGY" with great enthusiasm for establish-ing interspecies communication with the orca, and I believed then as now that it is possible. I think that I have solved the theoretical problem of communication with them, i.e., how they communicate, and accordingly how to communicate with them. But the closer I came to the plan the more doubts I developed as to whether it was right.

In the beginning all I could see was the positive benefits to cetaceans and humanity—and "all that dwells therein." My passion for orcas spilled over into the global problem of pre-serving cetaceans, and soon I was embroiled in international efforts to protect them.

Originally I had the right intentions, to help whales, to help humans help whales by "proving" that whales are aware, sen-tient, intelligent, compassionate and good beings, which is what I thought communicating with them linguistically would do. I also believed that such a "breakthrough" would help humanity become more aware, sentient, intelligent, compassionate and good. These intentions are fine but they are not the answer.

If we were to talk to dolphins or orcas, they might tell us what we already know but wish to ignore—that we need to be more compassionate, loving beings, that we are lost in the illusions of desire and fear, that we are attached to our egoic goals, that the real meaning of life is limitless joy, inner peace. The dolphins and orcas have been my teachers, and they offer their lessons to us by example— talking with them is not necessary to learn from them. Any dolphin watcher is moved by their very presence; they communicate the joy of being to all, and their reputation as compassionate beings is legion because it is true.

I see no real additional value in linguistic communication with them. It is clear to the open heart and mind that already they are master communicators and teachers. Now, what would happen to them if we were to establish linguistic communication? The governments of the world would coerce them into slavery, as some including ours already have, and the profiteers would capture and propagate them for all kinds of uses and abuses from medical technology to fisheries management and exploitation of the seas. They would become extensions of our egoic goals which already threaten their survival and environment.

We should want for the dolphins what we want for ourselves, to be free, peaceful, joyful, fearless, and trusting. To save the world, we must save ourselves. As Lao Tzu said, "If you would save the world look first to yourself." The dolphins require enlightenment from us far more than conversation with us.

19

Ethics:
More Rethinking Lilly

ESPITE THE ADVENT OF SOCIOBIOLOGY in the middle 1960s, followed by its rise to prominence as the New Darwinism during the 1970s, Lilly is still stuck on the "survival of the species." That may have been alright for Marlin Perkins, but for a scientist meeting the challenge of understanding the behavior of highly social species with which he hopes to talk, ignorance of the penetrating insights of sociobiology is a sorry thing. It is quite untrue, as Lilly states, that present biology views non-human behavior as lacking responsibility or help for others (conspecifics); the science of sociobiology is principally devoted to the phenomenon of cooperation among animals and humans, and it applies its general theory equally to both. A man should not say what a science does not say unless he knows what it does say. Especially when that science provides intellectual tools useful for identifying why and how societies, cooperation, language and behavior evolve.

In his chart comparing the human, Tursiops (bottle-nosed

dolphin—the Flipper type), and the orca, Lilly states that neither the dolphin nor the orca capture other species for sport, entertainment or education of their own species. Again, we find Lilly to be either ignorant of common knowledge among cetologists and biologists, or choosing to ignore concrete information in favor of promoting the delphinids in the eyes of humans. His strategy seems to be one of presenting the whales as conducting themselves in ways which humans would consider to be ethical for themselves, perhaps more ethical than humans. There are many documented examples to contradict Lilly's chart. As example, Nick Webb has described the wild but friendly dolphin, Beaky, who frequented England's harbors for several years, to repeatedly catch and release fish which he did not eat. I have watched orcas play with sea lions the way cats sometimes do mice, throwing them in the air, playing ball with the frightened creatures which they tossed hither and yon with their tail flukes. A well known National Geographic story photographically records the same thing, and there are documentary films of orcas teaching their young how to catch seals in the surf, again, much like a mother cat presenting opportunities for her kittens to use and perfect their inherited hunting skills. The orcas I observed did not eat the sea lions they played with, and the mother orca in the surf caught seals and released them for her youngster to chase; she did not kill or eat them.

Possibly the most dramatic instance of apparent teaching of young by orcas was observed and filmed by a National Geographic film crew. A group of orcas attacked but did not kill a sixty feet long, young blue whale. The adult bulls each grabbed a side of the blue whale's fluke as adult cows held the pectoral fins and then the young orcas proceeded to take mouthfulls of flesh out of the whale's body, creating, when they were apparently through, a six feet cubical wound with the appearance of having been made with surgical precision. The impression of the seasoned naturalists and photographers present, including at least one noted whale authority, was that the adults were educating the young orcas how to safely hold fast and feed on a great whale. So dangerous is a large whale to individual orcas that only by highly coordinated behavior could they attack them at low risk. It is precisely this kind of situation that would favor not only language-like communication for use in the attack and kill, but also to prepare youngsters by instruction.

In a chart comparing humans and dolphins, Lilly says under Ethics that humans are, "Human centered: no other species directed," and as for dolphins, "Dependence on others: no aggressivity, no hostile attacks." It simply is not true that humans do not include other species within their ethical systems. That the vast majority of humans do not maintain the same ethical posture to all beings equally should not surprise any one; however, that does not mean that humans have no ethics regarding other species. African pygmies' ethics include a tabu against killing pregnant cow elephants, for instance, and just because they hope to encourage the birth and development of elephants as a source of food for themselves does not mean that this ecologically self-serving code is unethical. It's easy to forget that, whatever the pygmies' intentions, they are also serving the interests of cow elephants and their unborn babies.

The American Indians upheld quite strict rules of conduct in relationship to the animals they hunted. The hunter needed to be right-minded, unegotistical in his quest, cleansed and purified both spiritually and physically, and he needed to take specific steps aimed at soliciting the animal's forgiveness. One may argue against such rituals as being self-serving in their purpose, but while they contain a recognition and explicit admission of the hunter's need for the animal as food, they effectively regulate human predation and tend to prevent overexploitation of animal resources. The Indians also adhered to strict conceptions about animal cruelty: if a hunter ever contributed to the unnecessary suffering of an animal he might pay severely in the future, for example, disease or poor health. Implicit in such ethics is the recognition that harmful thoughts and harmful deeds had karmic consequences, which is another

way of saying that the Indians really did see their lives as connected to nature.

The nature-sensitive philosophies of the east may tend to
discourage the killing of animals by humans, solely because it is
considered unethical for a human to interrupt the evolutionary
development of sentient life, all of which is viewed as sharing
the same ultimate path as humanity. But, whether such ethics
in fact do as much to insure the integrity and health of ecosys-
tems and the diversity of biotic communities as the ethics of
the hunters is doubtful. That one may refrain from killing cows
but devastate the habitat on which cows depend is contradicto-
ry; likewise, to give cows free reign on the landscape is to
discourage those wild species of large mammals with which
cows compete for forage. The systematic effects of various peoples' ethical beliefs about animals and nature may not turn out
to be positive for animals and nature, even for the people, but
that is not the point of contention here. What I am insisting
upon is that we take stock in the fact that people everywhere
throughout time and space hold ethical attitudes toward non-
human lifeforms.

That contemporary, industrialized societies in general may
not share Lilly's perception of and ethical conduct towards dolphins and whales is obvious, but that those same societies lack
ethics regarding animals is a ridiculous assertion: we have
scores of morals and laws about what constitutes proper conduct in relationship to non-humans. These vary from narrowly
self-serving codes such as punishment of horse thieves to regulation of animal capture to health standards for farm and zoo
animals to the earth conscious mandate to save endangered
species. I would be the first to admit that the present state of
affairs is miserable in so many respects, but, fundamentally, it is
universally human to relate to non-humans ethically.

Lilly's claims for Tursiops as having "Dependence on others:
no aggressivity, no hostile attacks," is as short-sighted as his
claim that humans are "no other species directed." Humans are
entirely dependent on other species, though many members of

industrialized civilization are ignorant and unappreciative of this and other vitally important facts of their existence. Neither is it so that Tursiops are unaggressive; they are to one another, and sometimes to other cetaceans upon whom they have dealt fatal attacks. Assuming that Lilly knows better than to lump predation with aggression, the proclivity of several delphinids to attack and kill sharks is legion. They do so not to feed themselves, nor always to defend young against a threat of immediate attack, but often to kill the sharks. Why? For the same basic reasons that humans around the world tend to kill larger predators, which, though not necessarily menacing in the present, may pose a danger in the future. Attacking and killing potentially threatening predators must qualify as interspecies aggression and hostility.

It is true that delphinids are not aggressive to humans, but a relatively small number of humans are aggressive to a great number of dolphins and other cetaceans, but that is not what Lilly said, and if it were true that humans are entirely self-centered then people such as Lilly and myself must be non-human. Kidding aside, the reason Hollywood built a fantasy after Lilly's work, Day of the Dolphin, and the reason that film was relatively successful is ample proof that humans are not strictly human centered. If they were, I wouldn't be writing this essay in the first place and you wouldn't be reading it.

Though interesting and important differences exist between species, which is the best reason to understand and try to learn from cetaceans, it is equally valuable to recognize that all living things share certain basic qualities. That humans want to survive or help kin survive is universal not only to humans but to all living things, and here we do not diverge from elephants, tigers, or whales; how some cetaceans have evolved to solve their vital problems is precisely what we may stand to learn from them.

As for ethical questions, Lilly attacks "The basic assumption ...that no other species have rights such as those of humans," unable to see that this is no mere assumption but a fact of life for humans and other species. That it is a fact is not to evaluate it: it simply is true, and life as we know it would be totally disrupted and destroyed if there were such a thing as biotic egalitarianism. Imagine the consequences of imposing human rights equally across the board for every lifeform: no car could be driven, no house built, no one could walk across their yard from fear of stepping on all sorts of organisms, dolphins would starve to death, so would every predatory species and every herbivore for that matter. Now, I am not saying that dolphins or gray whales do not deserve protection, nor that the sea should not be carefully looked after; I am saying that we cannot afford to skirt the fact that humans rule the planet and its destiny. Humans kill and consume whales for the same reasons that other humans resist whaling: in both cases, the behavior of humans is governed by self-interests. Whalers and anti-whalers are equally authentic; the problem is a matter of resolving who is likely to gain or lose what in the long-haul. Lilly and myself agree, on different philosophical grounds, that more humans stand to gain more by protecting and understanding whales, and the vitality of the seas, than by continuing to kill whales and pollute the seas. Conflicts of interest remain, of course, owing to the fact that what may be better for the whole or in the long-run, is not necessarily better for everyone, which is why well reasoned arguments are apt to win the day for whales.

However much so many people should like to think otherwise, there are no animal rights per se, but only rights given to animals by humans. This constitutes the only genuine ethical basis for saving or destroying anything. To promulgate "animal rights" as being inalieable to animals is the zenith of wayward idealism, and as such, could never be effective. I am not arguing against rights for animals, I am insisting that we need recognize that we shall dole out rights to non-humans as we see fit for whatever reasons we value. There need be no reconsideration of basic assumptions behind human relationships with whales: what we need is a new cost/benefit analysis in light of what Lilly and others believe can be gained by protecting them.

I have written at length elsewhere about the changing attitudes of humans toward animals and nature, which, of course, is a revision in basic assumptions, but it is no less in human interests to do so, and in fact it may be essential for human and planetary survival.

The Scientist

Lilly believes that those involved in interspecies communication research "should be least impeded by other scientists, by society," however, his meaning is not clear. Does this statement imply that Lilly feels his work has been so impeded? Certainly it is rare that scientists overtly impede one another, but at the covert level, as in review of grant proposals or manuscripts, they do impede scientific progress into novel areas. Perhaps Lilly has become hardened and defensive after years of intellectual intolerance. In truth, science as professionalism is ever more conformistic and competitive, and because it is professionalized, creativity is curtailed and discouraged. I know full well what Lilly has faced, and any free-thinking person in science may empathize with Lilly. Tremendous courage and a certain amount of healthy detachment is needed for anyone who crosses the threshold of the unknown; otherwise, they are apt to doubt themselves and their creative imagination, develop resentment and finally stifle their own contributions.

In the last part of Lilly's review of his work, his eye turns abruptly elsewhere in essays on scientific observation, legal status and perception of whales, and the scientist as "participant in ecology of the planet Earth." Though wandering from the book's theme, these topics are especially relevant to still unresolved questions about cetacean intelligence and its bearing on the "ethics of killing whales." Despite the claims of such groups as the International Whaling Commission, a self-appointed body of whaling managers transforming themselves into whale protectors, the international condition of most great whales is abominable and hardly anything has been done to help the smaller species such as the dolphins and the orca.

It is not likely, as Lilly says, that the modern scientific observer has, "evolved from conflicts between different human groups espousing different belief systems." More probable is Einstein's view, shared by anyone who has scrupulously investigated hunting societies, that science is a modern extension of evolutionarily ancient adaptations. Irrespective of inter-group relationships, so-called primitive societies conduct science routinely. Science is after all nothing but the mental construction of a hypothesis to solve a problem, and the hypothesis is tested by prediction about the outcome in actual experimentation, controlled or not. Like all of human life, science is problem-solving, which has been formalized and refined in modern societies.

We must disagree, too, with Lilly's view that the setting for early science was related to the dominance of mass-society religion, referring to the "Piscean Age," which started about 2,000 years ago and which is just now passing away. Prior to this era, there existed libraries, such as the one in Alexandria, containing as much as one million volumes, the literature and sciences of widespread intellectual schools and traditions with world views comparable to or exceeding those of modern science, including theories of life (natural selection) and the universe (the atomic theory, the world as round, understanding of the Van Allen belts, and so on). It was in this golden age that humans also may have recognized dolphins as mentally advanced creatures.

Lilly goes so far as to say that "in ancient religious teachings, man's brain was not understood," which is rather like saying that the first discovery of the circulation system was by Harvey. Chinese medicine thoroughly understood circulation at least five thousand years ago, not to mention that every extant hunting society knows quite well the operation of heart and vessels, where they are in the body and how to utilize this knowledge to deliver weapons most effectively for killing different species. There are European cave paintings about twenty-thousand years old which depict in red the heart and major arteries of large game animals. At least one function of such art may have been teaching young hunters where to strike the circulatory system. Prior to the nearly total destruction of the Pagan wisdom, the ancient religious teachings understood the human brain, as did Chinese medicine (acupressure). The examples of Native Americans employing brain surgery successfully are legion in anthropology.

The knowledge of the primitives and ancients about brains is not the crucial objection; rather, we must take argument with Lilly's notion that knowing something about brains actually constitutes world-shaking knowledge. That brains may function as holograms is earth shaking for the modern world, which has lost touch with the ancient wisdom, but before this recent insight, I am not sure that anything learned about brains has had any momentous consequences for anyone but the scientists claiming otherwise. And, the holographic view of brain function merely breathes life into the ancient views that physical organs are but one of several levels of being, that the brain is a physical channel for the non-physical mind, and so on.

Lilly further confuses his view of science by equating the objective brain with the personal subject's internal life. This is surprising in light of the fact that neurophysiologists were among the first scientists to philosophically distinguish the mind from the brain. But, not Lilly, who sounds more like a firm materialist-mechanist. He says that a scientist cannot be a neutral observer unless he, "has learned the structure of his own central nervous system." Taking him at his word, we could say that Gallileo, Newton, Darwin, Einstein and virtually every great scientist were incapable observers. It is one thing to expect self-observation and introspection to learn the structure of consciousness and thought; it is quite another to equate self or one's mind to the brain, which is not consciousness but a thing. We would be surprised if Lilly had ever observed his brain, but even if he had, we wonder exactly how his observation of his brain would inform him more than observation of himself (his consciousness). It is impossible to move from study of the brain to internal or subjective reality, as Lilly pretends; perhaps we should describe his philosophy as "pious neurologism."

Conservation

Despite widespread belief that whaling has ceased, it has not, and from all appearances probably will not in the immediate future. That some species or populations of great whales are receiving protection by unenforced treaty agreements is largely due to the fact that it is no longer profitable to kill them. And whales continue to be slaughtered, while others have never received as much as consideration for protection. The delphinids especially continue to be massacred around the world. Even the U.S. government allowed a "quota" of thousands of dolphins to be killed annually by the tuna industry when the mandate of the American people in the 1972 Marine Mammal Protection Act clearly intends that no cetaceans will be killed intentionally or "incidentally" for any commercial purpose.

After agreeing to cease killing the great whales, except for native subsistence in Siberia, which the Greenpeacers subsequently found to be done for fur ranches, the Russians "harvested" thousands of orcas in the Antarctic. They did not violate any agreements because nobody had thought to extend protection to orcas, though even if they had, many nations would have resisted. Fishermen in Scandanavia, for instance, view orcas as competitors for their fish, meaning the fish they sell to others for a profit, and they have rounded orcas up in coves and killed them en masse. The Japanese fishermen of Iki Island have turned their waters red with the blood of dolphins because they believe that the dolphins take their fish, again, not fish the men need for their subsistence, but which they sell on the market. And the Japanese seem irrevocably bent on funding a bankrupt whaling industry that threatened the North Pacific sperm whale as an expression of their national autonomy and cultural pride. One could elaborate ad infinitum on all the reasons why killing whales is rampant and why it is apt to continue. Even if it didn't, what humans are doing to destroy the vitality of the sea amounts to the same thing.

Already we may have reduced populations of some species to a critical threshold which may mean a continuing decline and extinction. That the bowhead whale has not seemed to recover from the Yankee whaling days is a major source of concern to Eskimo whaling. No longer required for subsistence, bowhead whaling is central to Eskimo culture. In the late 1970s, the whale experts were saying that the North Pacific sperm whales were not reproducing, that young calves were not appearing with cows, and that if the trend were to continue the population could die out. Perhaps the extreme overkill of sperm whales by the Japanese and Russians had somehow brought an abrupt cessation to mating or reproduction by the North Pacific sperm whales. Who knows what devastating impact the killing of just a few orcas may have on an entire group, that perhaps vitally adaptive knowledge important to the group's survival was erased with the capture of even a single member such as Namu? And who can say what global effects may result from the drastic decline of cetaceans owing to their ecological roles, as yet inadequately understood?

We pray for the realization of Lilly's prophecy; until then let us repeat his plea,

"Let us at least explore the possibility that they are capable in ways that we, in our present ignorance, cannot yet know about. The least we can do is stop killing them."

Many Russian scientists not only accepted Lilly's general thesis, they proceeded to pursue intensive projects on delphinid behavior and intelligence. Unlike most western scientists they seem to lack the tabu on using the word intelligence in reference to non-humans. Subsequent to Lilly's 1960 book, *Man and Dolphin*, which was translated into Russian, the Russians fully protected dolphins in the Black Sea and Sea of Azor, though dolphins previously had been taken as food. Nearly thirty years later, Lilly was still pleading for full protection of dolphins by the U.S., so as to assure their cooperation with us. Simultaneously, some esteemed western "cetologists" are dismissing any possibility of dolphin intelligence. The International Whaling Commission has, for the first time, considered the possibility of cetacean intelligence and though it has encouraged the cessation of whaling, dolphins and their kind remain unprotected. I think it is clear that however the conquest of outer space fares for the west, in the inner space of the ocean, and the inner space of the mind and heart, we have fallen behind.

RANDALL L. EATON

Orca back-breaching in Johnstone Strait, 1985.

'...the dolphin is really a human'

JOHN JHONNY IS FROM PONAPE, MICRONESIA. He had been studying in the U.S. for three years, and I was his teacher and advisor. Handsome, athletic, quiet and serious, John identified with my values. He wanted to return to Ponape to teach young adults that everything of meaning could be found right there. He had learned that big cars, making money and watching TV were not the answer. John missed the close-knit clan life, the palm wine, swimming inside the reef and fishing. He came to recognize that his home was rich, and that the sea held great promise for his people. During his life the old ways had begun to die, giving way to materialism. The Japanese were raping the environment, and the last Kahunas were dying off with no disciples to follow them.

John's father was visiting, and he came to my office to talk with me, John and Estephan, John's uncle and fellow student at the college, about our plan to develop a marine resource program in Ponape. We sat and talked about fishing, our common love of the sea, how beautiful she is, and finally we talked about the dolphins that come inside the reef every day. John said,

"The reef, oh, it is so alive. That's where I fish. Oh, yeah, we have legends like that, too. That the dolphin is really a human. It's tabu to kill a shark back there. Like you said, because there's this tabu form [tabu variant]. One name for the shark on land, its real name, and another, like King would be be in English. A lord of the sea, you know. But it's like you said about lions and bear signs and trophies, because people, they fear the sharks. Sure. But they think the dolphins and whales they are good luck. When you see them and you're fishing everyone says that means good luck.

"Yeah, there is also a shark clan [one of five on the island]. They seem to be in touch with the sharks, someway. There's many stories about people there, drowning out to sea, and shark, he saved them. Many stories like this. Yeah, they say that my relative, she was an old lady then, she thought she was drowning at sea but a big old shark brought her on his back to shore. Many people saw it they say. I don't know if I believe it, but there are many stories. The men, some of them fishermen, they catch sharks, and it's like the robe that that Hercules wore, the lion's mane you told about. The people they put the biggest shark, the jaws with the teeth, they hang them up over their doors, you know. To show everybody. Everybody knows then they got a big shark. And it stays up there long time, too.

"But the whales and dolphins, leave them alone alright. Back there the people they say that its not right to kill a dolphin. Cause, well, its kind of hard to say, but they say they are just like human. Like us. And only once did I know anyone to eat them. There was this guy, a fisherman, he's a distant relative of mine [nearly everyone is related on Ponape]. He's not a good guy. I went to his house once to eat, and there was all this red meat on the counter. Piles of it, stacks, like this. But I didn't know what it was so I just sat down and ate dinner with them. Like always. So it was real nice and everything but then I stopped and said to him, 'Hmmm, what is this I'm eating,' and he told me it was dolphin and...I couldn't help it. I had to get up and go out of there...I mean get away from there fast. And I puked, I couldn't help it. Man, it was awful. And I never went back there. Never. That guy, he was wrong to do that. For me it was just like eating a person. I felt so bad. You know, I should not have eaten that dolphin. I am ashamed to say that man is my relative. I tell him that, too."

The Ponapean Government made a deal with the Japanese, allowing them to come inside the reef and fish as much as they like, and of course the Japanese took virtually everything from shellfish to dolphins. In return the Ponapeans received, supposedly, 10% of the profits from the catch. Rather than develop and conserve their marine resources, the Ponapeans were throwing them away for a few thousand dollars annually. The young people of John and Estephan's generation are not staying in Ponape to fish or work in fisheries management or the viable tourism/diving industry, but instead are heading out to the states for an "education," and part-time jobs that translate into used Thunderbirds and modern houses in tract developments—the American dream. But only a few such as John and his father, who laments ever leaving the sea to go to work for the Government, will see beyond the Yankee illusion. Their relative is still breaking an ancient tabu and eating dolphins, and his Government is trading dolphin flesh for money.

21

For the Love of
a Tuna Fisherman,
Or How to Save a Dolphin

AT AN EMERGENCY CONFERENCE called in Seattle to avert conflict between the federal government and the native Alaskans over their threat to kill more bowhead whales than the quota allowed, I interviewed a high-ranking NOAA official about the dolphin-tuna problem. He was extremely proud that his agency had succeeded in establishing lower quotas for the incidental kill of dolphins from drowning in the nets of tuna fishermen. Since the Marine Mammal Protection Act is a public mandate to protect all whales and dolphins, and his agency was supposed to enforce official policy aimed at achieving a zero kill by the tuna fishery, I asked him why the quota wasn't zero. His demeanor switched from smugness to visible irritation. "Why can't you people see what a hell of a job we've done? What do we have to do? Year by year, we've reduced the quotas, and next year there'll be only fifteen to twenty thousand killed."

He carefully explained to me that it was just a small handful of tuna boats of one or two companies which accounted for almost all the dolphin kill. The vast majority had adopted fishing techniques that prevented the drowning of dolphins taken accidentally in the nets. He added that the complying fishermen who were abiding by the law "resented the few mavericks," which made sense considering that the culprits were giving the good guys a bad name, even diminishing their long-range material prospects in the event that public outcry was severe enough. I asked why his agency didn't crack down on the culprits. He knew who the bad guys were, and he'd already admitted that they were violating federal codes he was entrusted to enforce. His reply was slippery bureaucratese, "We have to be very careful not to frighten all the fishermen into thinking we're going to make sacrificial lambs of them. We need their cooperation and trust if we're going to be able to solve the problem. If we go in and bust the abusers, we might panic the whole fleet, and then we'd never get their cooperation."

I reminded him that the good guys would be happy to have him get the culprits, that such a move would be in their interest and could make everyone happy. He couldn't see it. My guess is that his real concern was about publicity that would result from his agency busting the culprits since it might inspire a new wave of people boycotting tuna and that might mean that the good fishermen would suffer unnecessarily. And if the whole fishery's economy suffered there would be political pressure against him personally, which could mean he'd lose his position. I've yet to meet a high-ranking bureaucrat charged with managing natural resources of any kind whose principle ethos wasn't cover your ass first, never step on anyone's toes and walk the middle of the road until overwhelming force moves you one way or the other.

Dolphins don't vote, and even if in the cosmic picture they are the equivalent or superior of humans, beings who could teach us much about love, about proper relationship among the kingdoms, how to use and care for the ocean, and God knows what else, our government allowed a few greedy tuna fishermen to continue killing them by the thousands because a clever bureaucrat lacked the courage to take a less than earth-shaking step that would end the problem at once. Perhaps he was on the take or simply stupid, but one thing is sure: until each and every one of us is willing to make the personal sacrifices appropriate to right action, things will only get much worse before they get better. By whatever means necessary, the universe is a self-correcting system, which is why we must pity the NOAA official on whose head rest the needless deaths of thousands of dolphins.

To protect dolphins, my students were actively promoting the boycott of tuna as well as all Japanese products to protect whales. They plastered walls and car bumpers with stickers, "Save the whales—boycott Japanese products" and "Save the dolphin—Boycott tuna." In their revolutionary zeal, still alive from the sixties among the "whale hippies," they had become attached to their advocacy. They were angry and hateful. I told them that if they wanted to solve the problem of dolphins being killed by humans they would have to love tuna fisherman as much as the dolphin, that saving dolphins meant extending love to consumers of tuna and buyers of Japanese cars and radios.

Being the only faculty member whom they felt deserved their allegiance until then, I was not surprised nor sorry that they decided to drop me from their list of gurus—John Lilly, Tom Wolfe, Timothy Leary and the Grateful Dead.

On the side of right it isn't always obvious that enthusiasm fired by anger over the way of the world is the same motivation that kindles war and every form of human division including that with the environment and creatures. To love what is right is one thing, but to let that proper love become egotistical desire is to automatically invite fear of failing to satisfy desire, which in turn means division, resentment and hate. My students' love for dolphins became unknowingly transformed into hate for tuna fishermen and the Japanese, just as the NOAA official's fear of upsetting the good fishermen or losing his job stood in the way of his love and right action. When our thoughts and actions are not founded on love but ego, the resources of the heart are inflamed and dissipated. Genuine disobedience or protest is precisely peaceful. Our lesson is one of learning to point to what in our heart of hearts we feel is right without resenting those who disagree. And fully trusting love no matter what. *The energy behind our actions ultimately governs its consequences.*

There is no doubt that in terms of what we humans have to gain, we owe it to ourselves and the world to protect dolphins and whales. My students learned that they could boycott tuna and love the tuna fisherman, and I am confident that the NOAA official easily could have convinced the maverick fishermen that it was completely in their interest to stop killing dolphins.

Enlightened self-interest in the meaning of the Buddha or Aristotle is the singular method by which human life progresses and evolution occurs. Our educational process as stewards of all that moveth upon the earth must involve self-love and self awareness, which nurtures ego transcendence, the provision for changing the world to a better world, the commitment and revelation that is Life.

22

Do Sperm Whales Feel Pain
When Bombs Explode
In Their Bodies?

THE GREAT WHALES is a splendid film produced by National Geographic in which appears footage shot by Greenpeace confronting a Russian whaling boat in pursuit of North Pacific sperm whales. It is by far the most remarkable statement yet made about the mentality of whales and humans.

As the huge whaler closes in on the fleeing pod of sperm whales consisting of one bull in the lead of a tightly packed group of mature females, two Greenpeacers in an inflatable align themselves between the harpoon boat and the whales. Assuming that the Russians will not risk killing them with a shot, they take their raft right up to the last whales until they are nearly on top of a cow. The sperm whales are porpoising, their fastest mode of travel, indicating that they are much afraid.

The man on the bow behind the gun fires immediately over the heads of the men in the raft. The harpoon disappears into the body of the last cow, explodes and turns the water red with blood. Then the most unexpected thing happens: the bull turns around and swims right by the raft, ignoring it, directly to the whaling boat. He comes full-length straight up out of the water, his jaws open and pointed at the prow. The cannoneer shoots an explosive bomb into the massive brain of the sperm whale, apparently killing it instantly.

Are sperm whales merely big fish—a term used to describe the orca by an employee of the National Marine Fisheries Service—controlled by blind instincts, incapable of reasoning or complex problem solving? Could anyone doubt that the bull sperm whale knew precisely what he was doing? That it was the big ship behind him, not the closer, motored craft, which fired a deadly weapon at one of his herd. That the enemy was not the closest human or human craft nor the hull of the whaler but none other than the man behind the cannon high above the water, a man and gun that by all appearances the bull could not possibly have observed until after the harpoon was fired.

It has been said the amount of reason in a human being can be measured in an eye dropper. How else are we to explain the fact that our scientists and moral philosophers devote endless rhetoric to the question of whether or not whales experience pain when bombs explode in their bodies? As recently as 1980, the fate of the world's whales was placed in such a context at the International Whaling Commission's Conference On the Intelligence of Cetaceans and *the Ethics of Killing Them* (my emphasis).

Whether in terms of science or common sense it would seen that things have changed little in the unlovely human mind over 300 years. As the Age of Reason overtook Europe, experimentation in physiology became popular and animals including dogs were nailed to laboratory walls and dissected. As the animal cried out, squeamish students were assured that it felt no pain, that what appeared to be painful was simply the consequence of a mechanism like the spring in a clock being manipulated.

Cartesianism would have us believe that our human egos are the only undeniable reality in the world, and that all non-humans are but blind machines incapable of feeling or consciousness. And most of us are convinced that we are incapable of experiencing directly another organism's pain. The version of this philosophy so pervasive in science and contemporary society, despite the radically different world view that has emerged in this century from physics, is mechanism. Which conveniently accounts for everything in the universe and how it works or functions, everything that is but the scientist himself.

Mechanism is actually a projection of the human ego's insatiable desire for power and control over the world including other humans ("them"), but after so many years of successful manipulation, we no longer think mechanism, it thinks us. And in thinking us, mechanism, insulates us from the world, virtually eliminating grand spectrums of communication with one another, other creatures and non-physical forces and beings. Our rampant egoism is the real culprit of course; it is the bicep that contracts awareness so severely that we experience but a fraction of what our innate capabilities offer. When Shakespeare wrote that there is more in heaven and earth than is dreamt of in our philosophy, he summarized the predicament of the modern soul, drowning in human arrogance, and he also prophesied the new physics' ethic of humility.

Nowhere are we more blatantly lost than in our perception of the human/animal connection. The prevalent attitude towards communication with animals is derived from this Neo-Cartesian argument: since we cannot know with certainty the subjective life of another human or animal, then it is only possible to infer from objectively observed behavior what the human or animal may think or feel. In another word, reality is that which can be measured—for "proof"—and nothing more.

Unknowingly, most of us have completely convinced ourselves of this belief system, and thereby managed to reject actual experience to the contrary. As a consequence we maintain defensive ego-consciousness within its fragmented realm and refuse to challenge in thought or on the basis of experience this unproved and unprovable assumption. Though I may be wrong, for now at least I am convinced that I have experienced immediately and directly another being's pain. Now it is risky, of course, to say such things in print because "scientists" are not supposed to ever disagree too much with prevailing views, but, for whatever it is worth I offer as my defense the words of Albert Einstein that we owe it to ourselves and everyone else to always say exactly what it is we believe.

I was sitting in plane geometry class at the high school when suddenly I yelled and grabbed my foot which felt like it was burning. The arch of my left foot hurt terribly and all I could do was sit and hold it, bear the pain and sweat. After several minutes, about five, the sharp pain and burning sensation subsided and class returned to normal. After class let out I was walking down the hallway when Marsha Whitten stopped to ask if I were going to the hospital...my brother had shot himself in the arch of the left foot with my shotgun at about 10:40 AM, the time when I yelled and grabbed my left foot. At the hospital he described the sensation of the blast without knowing what I had experienced in class; he said, "It felt like my foot was on fire"... the same adjective I'd used.

Being thoroughly trained—which really means indoctrinated—in behavioral science, I know well the ready questions and criticisms. And though I could respond by pointing out that never before or since have I had such a sensation anywhere in my body (nor has my brother so traumatized himself before or since), and though my brother and I could agree to polygraphic analysis or hypnotism to verify our claims. nothing we could say or do would qualify as sufficient evidence for the mechanist. The best assessment would be "mere coincidence." There is nothing "mere" to any coincidence, since co-incidental phenomena in an interdependent, ordered universe are precisely what makes science possible; however, science prefers to adhere to its self-serving myths. It is sad that non-physicists among scientists are not more aware of what the new physics means for science and humanity, and the biologists seem most conservative in this regard. Many individuals including great figures in the history of science have claimed experiences comparable to my own which defy mechanistic explanation, and dismissing them as mere coincidence is as absurd as Cartesianism itself. That science does not permit a method by which such experiences may be empirically verified is no valid excuse for ignoring them, and to continue doing so for much longer will mean either that science must evolve or it will become widely recognized as valid only within its self-proclaimed province, which will be seen as a shrinking segment of reality...the times, as they say, are changing.

Besides, there is a huge body of scientifically impressive data in support of the theory that we humans possess faculties that would allow inter-individual communication of subjective experiences. The data pertaining to animal-human psychic communication are also compelling; for now the mainstream of science finds it simply more convenient to ignore them for the sake of upholding the false security of its world view. Which, try as we may to deny it, is what retards human progress on every front. We are in desperate need of a new philosophy, one with courage.

The Cartesian paradigm is responsible for much of our pain and suffering, and that pain and suffering further reinforces our belief in Cartesianism, a vicious circle of egoism. We delude ourselves into believing that we are separate from the world, alone, in the hope that this will protect us from the world when, in fact, all it does is establish psychic barriers which cut us off from one another and other creatures, leaving us in the position of resisting not only pain and suffering— which creates far more of it, but increasing alienation and its ills: stress, conflict, war, materialism, greed, and everything that terribly besets us in the social and ecological realms.

Perhaps this regrettable, self-reinforcing pattern of self and world destruction is simply the consequence of humans finding themselves living in mass society, which, in terms of human needs may as well be termed non-society. We are removed from the interdependent life of true societies in which every one is well known, the rules of conduct are clear or spontaneously corrective, a life which, essentially, provides genuine social security by placing individuals in authentic relationships to one another and society as a whole. True social life encourages individuality because each individual has transpersonal significance. Individualism inevitably is defined socially.

True societies exist as far as I know only in primal situations where humans depend on one another and they are fully conscious of their dependence on nature. For the primal human, life is defined by his dependence on spirit, the group and on the environment, and where ego is interdependent with the world, rampant egoism is impossible; life is necessarily transcendent. Communication with spirit, other humans and with nature and her creatures and forces is the basic assumption. The shaman communicates with animals. and mistreatment of deer could bring havoc upon an individual from deer/nature spirits.

Sharp contrast with our life. We worship, praise and emphasize individuation, ego-consciousness, "aggressiveness," competition, status and wealth, everything we don't need and which accounts for our head-long rush to destruction. Is it any wonder we can't talk to the animals? That our scientists sit in pretentious composure cautiously adhering to the Law of the Accepted, debating issues like Do Sperm Whales Feel Pain When Bombs Explode in Their Bodies? That in the name of "humane" treatment thousands of human lives are devoted to killing fifty million cats and dogs annually? That educated America argues that the Soviets are out to get us so we'd better keep building more nuclear weapons—after all, some insist, a nuclear war is survivable? That so-called Christians would rather strike first than turn the cheek? That a brush war in God only knows where gathers more attention than loss of ozone?

The question of how we treat animals is no different than how we treat other humans—or ourselves. All speak to one thing, our self-imposed resistance to life itself. For any of this to change we must first begin to face life head on, to accept what hurts along with what doesn't, admitting that our resistance causes enormous pain, suffering and misery. Attention and self-knowledge is the path out. Then we might discover that pain is not quite as painful as we imagined, that we may experience pain and be better for it, that life is not ego and self-defensiveness, but ego and the world in mutually interdependent transcendence, that such awareness constitutes freedom, and from it we become more loving, more intelligent, more human, and better able to meet the problems of this world in a healthy, positive light.

As long as humanity lives in fear it will incur fearful consequences: self-fulfilling prophesy. Fear exists in the hearts of men, almost all of it imaginary and invalid, and so it is awareness of the source of fear as the cause of our pain which may lead us home. Nothing else will do.

The revolution in the way we perceive and relate to animals represents nothing less than a philosophical transmutation from idealism or egoism to co-existence or transcendentalism. When one discovers in the quietude of a peaceful heart that neither he nor anything else is strictly mechanical, but that everything in the universe is truly alive, even in death, then fear, ego and self give way to love and Infinite Being, in whose body we live with the orcas, sperm whales, aphids and planets. Life, all of it is a Great Mystery. Awareness of the fact of living brings down the veils of illusion and initiates us into another kingdom, literally the Kingdom of Heaven. Fear is, it exists, but whether it rules our life is a question of commitment to awareness of it. Fear, too, is sacred, and here is a great secret—in loving our fear and pain we also transcend ourselves.

Then the magic begins.

23

The Natural History
of Professional Cetology

WRITTEN IN THE STYLE of a higher-ranking trophy hunter, The Natural History of the Whale not only defends the status quo, it also vehemently attacks professionally unaccepted ideas. The tone of the book is characterized by this quote in the preface:

"'Cetological literature is full of poorly supported conjecture.'"

How very applicable is this proclamation to the thought of the author, L. Harrison Matthews, who continually makes unfounded assertions declaring what cetaceans are not, a strategy usually considered beyond human intellect and best left to God.

There was a time when this book angered me more than any other because it reflects the blindness, stupidity and stubbornness of the professional protecting his narrow self-interests by thoughtlessly discounting new, different and non-professional ideas. The grave problem of conformity of thought in science exists because individuals compete for status in groups by conforming to accepted values, beliefs and ideas. I identify this sorry phenomenon as trophy hunting, and view it as the most serious impediment to human advance and welfare. Nowhere is professionalism more blatant than in cetology, a field in which the mechanistic mentality of scientists such as Matthews may have inhibited world-wide efforts to understand and preserve cetaceans.

Chapter four, on breeding and growth, begins with a startling passage indicative of an age of pious idealism:

"Feeding, however, is only a means towards reproduction, which is the main purpose of life, if life can be said to have any purpose."

Metaphysics aside, the principle of natural selection identifies feeding as adaptive or beneficial strictly in terms of how it influences reproductive success. And sociobiology, the contemporary version of natural selection, would say that all behavior, including cooperation or altruism, succeeds in so far as it serves individuals' interests (not groups'). Matthews is right then to say that reproduction is the primary purpose of life, but he qualifies this comment with, "if life can be said to have any purpose," which epitomizes the deep conflict in science and society.

Our selfish obsession with ideation and intellection, brought to a peak by the immense success of idealism and physics has resulted in a lack of awareness of ourselves and our biological motivation: survival and success, to follow, reproduce, the meaning implicit in "a better life." Better for whom? Our successors, of course. Universally, human values and efforts have a common yardstick—the survival and better life of succeeding generations. We are futurists at heart.

When our intellectuals fail to comprehend purpose in life we are in desperate straits. All the more pathetic that a biologist's most adhered to idea, natural selection, is not grasped as a statement of the fact of life as purpose. Should we force life into the Newtonian version of cause and effect on the billiard table, where ball strikes and moves ball purposelessly yet predictably, or should we take note of the fact that we ourselves, and by every measure all living organisms, are radically and irrevocably purposeful?

In his next paragraph we find illustration of the stifling effect of competition among intellectuals:

"It is not possible in the present state of knowledge to guess why the self-replicating DNA molecules should have produced such an enormous variety of living things to carry them as an endless stream for millions of years so that they are in effect immortal."

Why not natural selection? Isn't it the biological explanation for evolution of species? And, why is it not possible to guess? Perhaps Matthews means speculate or theorize. Our "present state of knowledge" is what we already believe is true; it was made by ceaseless guessing, speculating and theorizing—thinking in response to life's problems. Since our present state of knowledge is surely insufficient we had better guess. Scientists must stop clinging to facts—actually their beliefs and theories—in favor of questioning and imagining outloud for common consideration.

Science is one thing, the construction of theory, ideas, not the accumulation of doctrine in the disguise of "skepticism," which usually amounts to trophyism gone amuck. Open minds require open hearts: creative discovery, invention and problem solving rest on defenseless and fearless thinking, not playing it safe. We must, as Ortega says, learn to be second, third or last, which means that those whose vital mission it is to think cannot afford to conform their perception according to the cult's doctrines. If science is to fulfill its radical collective mission of helping us adapt to ourselves and our world then the scientists themselves will have to adopt the meta-method of self-awareness. Otherwise, science rightly should return to the amateurs, lovers of discovery unhindered by professionalism. A few amateurs come to mind: Leibnitz, Newton, Bacon, Mendel, Darwin and Einstein in his great period of youth, before, in his words, he was expected to lay golden eggs. The giants of western science and culture—like it or not science is our culture—were not professionals, and being free from the egotistical desire for success and fear of failure which more recent professional science demands, they were more creative. The "present state of knowledge" was not their god. Tragically, there is ample reason to suspect that they and their creations would never have come to the fore in our time, and were it not for his perspicacity and incredible courage, Einstein would have been washed out by the establishment, which made every effort to do so.

When a writer presents himself as an authentic scientist but implies that it is not within scientific propriety for him to guess due to strictures of present knowledge we should remind him of his freedom to reach beyond and to create. A healthy society cannot be content with accepting the inevitably destructive posture of worshipping the known and fearing the unknown; all the more so for our unhealthy society. So absorbed in their professional ambitions, scientists forget that the most important science, the only real scientific enterprise, is always those ideas in least agreement with the present state. If a writer is not a thinker, let him write, but do not believe with him that we cannot think.

Matthews reduces the "strong sexual inclinations" of male dolphins to mere neurosis. But even as neurosis we would like to know why these particular organisms are so prone to the affliction. In an effort to reduce cetaceans to simple machines, Matthews supports his neurosis argument for dolphin sexuality by relating penile stimulation in captive males to wild dolphins who have befriended people. He refers specifically to Beaky, a wild but friendly dolphin who frequented the coasts of England towing boats, giving free tows to children swimming at beaches and rubbing his penis against the bottom of boats. As well publicized in England as were the antics of Beaky, it's surprising that Matthews doesn't mention Beaky's efforts to pair with women, whom he harmlessly abducted while they swam offshore. Would mere neurosis account for the fact that Beaky did not abduct or sexually approach children or men?

Rather than admit what appears to be sexual conduct on the part of an adult male dolphin which parallels human sexual attitudes, all the more startling knowing that male dolphins typically behave sexually toward other males and juveniles, Matthews would have us dismiss Beaky's behavior as pathological. The assessment of many dolphin experts is that dolphins employ sexual gestures in much the same way that we use handshakes, back patting and the like, as expressions of affection, but Matthews would prefer the Cartesian view that all animals save man are blind automatisms incapable of feeling or reason.

And Matthews conveniently ignores widely known information that virtually all dolphins everywhere, not just captive males or wild, friendly dolphins like Beaky, are exceptionally sexual in their day-to-day social life. Should we consider the normal behavior of dolphins to be neurotic?

The usual cetological explanation for dolphins such as Beaky who are friendly to humans, is that they are probably social outcasts, supposed to imply that their loneliness accounts for an attraction to people. Equally widespread but wholly without support, is the view that wild, friendly dolphins must have escaped from captivity where they were socialized to people.

Since no one can possibly account for the disappearance from captivity of a social group of the particular species befriending people in Australia, the cetological explanation won't work. It is obvious, too, that these dolphins are not in need of companionship. But Matthews skirts the question of why any animal of a species frequently killed by humans would seek friendship with humans. It is an overwhelming fact that cetaceans are the only wild animals, and the toothed whales the only mammalian predators, which are ever friendly to humans upon or shortly after capture, without training or reinforcement of any kind. Imagine capturing an adult lion, wolf or bear which has not been tamed or socialized to humans. How would you expect one to behave towards people? The same applies to mice, pheasants, ducks and feral cats and dogs—all are extremely frightened or aggressively defensive. Indeed, humans captured by strangers are no different.

In most cases throughout history going back thousands of years in China, Arabia, and Greece, and for hundreds of years in Europe, America, New Zealand and Australia, it has been the cetaceans who have solicited friendly relations with humans, not vice-versa. "Interspecific altruism" with humans is unique among wild and untamed animals to cetaceans, and can hardly be ignored with the flimsy word neurosis.

Describing how females without calves "appear to cooperate with the mother in nudging it [the calf] to the surface," we learn from Matthews that this reaction is sometimes:

". . .misdirected to other objects, for dolphins or porpoises of several species have sometimes come to the assistance of human swimmers in difficulties and helped to support them to the surface. Such actions have, as might be expected, been recorded in romantic and anthropomorphic form by people who see more in the occurrence than is justified by the facts."

But what are the facts: that dolphins have saved human lives, throughout history and much of the world. With the facts in hand, what possible explanation is there? A biologist would use natural selection: individuals behave in ways that serve their self-interests. What might dolphins gain by spending valuable time and energy pushing humans ashore? They have gained from the human response of affection and cooperation, including reduction of human aggression, higher survival rates, and a growing world-wide concern for the destiny of dolphins and the salvation of their sea home. In the face of an overwhelmingly dominant and dangerous species which exploits common fish resources, there could not possibly be a more effective strategy.

In ancient and modern mythology, dolphins have earned a special place solely by their cooperative, friendly and non-violent behavior to humans. I mention non-violence because many delphinids, not only the killer whale, could easily kill humans in the water. That they don't is problematical. If for no other reason than the fact that humans prey on dolphins for food, slaughter them en masse for competing for fish, and overexploit their food resources, dolphins should kill humans when the risks are nil, which is often the case.

Not only are dolphins highly skilled predators, the equal of felines on land, they are quite capable of killing a water borne human with impunity. A male bottle-nosed dolphin weighing several hundred pounds moving at speeds over twenty knots could use its rock-hard beak to kill a human with a single blow. Dolphins often kill large sharks, of course, and employing their highly evolved cooperative tactics, they could be awesome against people. But they aren't, not even under circumstances in which we'd most expect it, including self-defense and defense of young. The horrifying photos of the Japanese fishermen of Iki Island walking waist deep in bloody water spearing and slicing hundreds of dolphins contained by nets is a prime example of the passivity of dolphins in relationship to humans. If the fishermen knew that the dolphins did not feed on the fish they catch, they wouldn't kill the dolphins, and if they realized that elsewhere in the Pacific, dolphins voluntarily help island fisherman herd fish into nets, they might not kill them, and if they were aware how readily the dolphins they kill unnecessarily could turn the water red with the fishermen's blood, perhaps they would understand that the dolphins know something infinitely more important than they or the biologist...that fish and survival itself are not as sacred as loving your brother.

The best biological explanation for dolphins saving humans when they receive no immediate gains—food, protection and so on—is that they stand to benefit in the long run. The same principle applies to lions when they attack and kill unmenacing hyenas but do not eat them, or to humans who tend to kill harmless predators because they might be harmful in the future. It is plausible that dolphins are aware not only that they stand to gain, but also that we are likely to respond cooperatively to their friendship?

The drama of dolphin and man is a beautiful case of reciprocity by communication of intentions dependent upon mutual awareness. Here is the message of the whale people, not the cetologists.

So important is this way of "thinking like a dolphin" that the usual objections deserve comment. We hear that since dolphins push mattresses and other human artifacts from ship wrecks to shore they must not be trying to save people. Meant here are two underlying objections: 1) if they push mattresses, dolphins simply must be mistaken robots—why push mattresses unless driven by what Matthews terms misdirected instinct? 2) if they consciously intended to save humans they wouldn't be so stupid as to rescue a bed.

If dolphins save human lives, for some kind of benefit, then it is reasonable that they would also save things valued by humans. And if this rescuing behavior were some raw, instinctive thing, why don't dolphins do it to other dolphins? Are we to entertain the notion that of all species, dolphins fail to discriminate between humans and other dolphins? Though the behavior of lifting calves or injured dolphins to the surface may be fundamentally instinctive, the taking-to-shore behavior could not be. Dolphins don't take untroubled humans to shore, and they never take other dolphins to shore, so they must be making some extremely fine discriminations about who should go to shore and why. Tell the Dutch helicopter pilot whose raft was pushed by a single dolphin in the same direction for a week safely to shore that dolphins are blind machines, hopelessly compelled to invest incredible time and energy rescuing humans. No such instinct conceivably could evolve.

Its significant that cetaceans other than dolphins and porpoises lift infants to the surface but they do not rescue humans or their property. Neither do any other lifeforms except tamed and domesticated animals for which gains can be identified.

When our radical rules do not conform with the world, we try to make them fit, make a better rule or admit we can't. Matthews makes no exceptions fit, neither does he follow his own rules; he merely dismisses important exceptions with terms fitting his trade, all to uphold an archaic value system in which the human ego reigns supreme on earth, everything else being but insensitive objects placed here for our indifferent use.

There is nothing more wonderful than the exquisite swimming and jumping of dolphins, whether in nature or captivity. Matthews invites wrath when he says:

"Thus what appears to us to be a joyful and sportive exhibition of high spirits is in reality nothing of the sort; contrary to the anthropomorphic interpretation it is merely a matter-of-fact necessity."

What necessity? Matthews does not propose any sort of explanation for the dolphin's exceptionally playful antics. Matthews employs the strictest form of empirical philosophy, which says, I can never know with certainty the internal life of any other being, including other humans, thus, I cannot say that the leaping dolphin is joyful, sportive or in high spirits. But then Matthews contradicts this rule. To apply it properly would mean that he cannot know that the dolphin is not joyful or sportive. Incidentally, several researchers have concluded that much delphinid jumping cannot be explained except as expression of exuberance. Humans and dolphins are among the most playful organisms, and, again, each offers a superb model for understanding the other.

Matthews persistently rejects anthropomorphism without realizing that he deceives himself: all interpretation by humans, all of science, and all language usage is inevitably anthropomorphic. If and when science is conducted without the direct or indirect participation of humans, it will no longer be anthropomorphic. Perhaps we shall find that delphinids conduct science, which, wouldn't surprise me one bit, and then we can speak about delphinomorphism and how dolphins ascribe their qualities to us. It might surprise us to learn, in this case, that they know us better than we know ourselves. Why? Because human evolution has meant both self-deception and deception of others, but owing to their use of sonar to monitor their aquatic world, a sensory system which penetrates objects including other individuals, delphinids and other sonar-using cetaceans may be incapable of lying.

Discussing migration, Matthews again discounts the possibility of cetacean intelligence and awareness, and for reasons not given discounts recognition of landmarks and navigation. Since baleen whales do not use sonar or echolocation, he says,

"Direct sound signals might be a possible method of following those that have gone ahead, because the sound emitted by cetaceans travels to great distances under water—but what of those at the front who have gone before them to give signals?"

Why not culture? Bluejays migrate by following established landmarks—patches of forest, farm buildings, orchards and so on—and the young birds rely on sight and sound to follow the older birds and learn the route from them. Mountain sheep depend on older individuals with previous experience to locate wintering grounds, and as many species pass on acquired information, it would seem incredulous that long-lived, large-brained cetaceans could not use culture to find their way. Matthews reduces cetacean migration to "built-in behavior," which, of course, it could be, but only in part for the wide-ranging social predators—delphinids, beluga and sperm whale—which must adjust movements according to fluctuations in food species.

However, Matthews asserts,

"It is inconceivable that cetaceans, or any other animals, have even the crudest sort of mental chart of any part of the oceans, and it is equally improbable that they can have any knowledge of where they are going or why."

It is quite inconceivable that any contemporary scientist or educated person could make this assertion: one might as well resort to the out-landish Cartesianism of 300 years ago. It is thoroughly documented that birds inherit mental charts of the heavens which they use to navigate. Why couldn't whales with relatively fixed directional and seasonal migration patterns inherit some sort of mental chart? The existence of an innately acquired navigational system does not in any way preclude learning or awareness. Sex in humans is basically an innately acquired drive or instinct, but that in no way precludes our awareness of sex nor the influence of experience or conscious will on its expression. What is patently clear is that cetaceans and scores of marine mammals and birds certainly seem to know precisely where they are going much of the time. Whether cetacean navigation is innately acquired or learned or both simply isn't known.

When Matthews reviews the awesome communication and echolocation of cetaceans, he presents much information supporting a view that these species are mentally advanced. But he prefers to attack such a view with unfounded negation:

"The hallucinations and fantasies of the enthusiasts who think that dolphins have a high level of intelligence and are able to communicate with each other and even with man by means of a well developed language are unsupported by any scientific evidence. It is unfortunate that these fallacious ideas have received much publicity and have been widely accepted by an uncritical public lacking the information and means of assessing their value."

There is an enormous amount of evidence supporting the idea that dolphins are highly intelligent and communicative. The scientific evidence indicates that they learn as quickly to solve discrimination problems as humans, and that their memories are comparable. It is also clear from scientific experiments that dolphins communicate complex problem-solving information with sound, and there are many reasons to believe that they have developed language or a communication system that achieves as much or more than language. Why is it that the National Science Foundation supports a leading cetacean psychologist's efforts to teach language to dolphins in Hawaii? Tell this leading scientific organization they are hallucinating and uncritical.

Anyone who has observed delphinids long or thought about their lifestyle will believe that they are extremely communicative and among the most socially developed species. Surprisingly, Matthews denies that they are cooperative:

"Schools of killer whales are sometimes referred to as 'packs,' thereby suggesting that the individuals in a school co-operate in pursuing their prey, and that their actions are the result of intelligence and foresight of the consequences. No one would suggest that Fin whales co-operate in attacking a shoal of planktonic krill, and there is no reason for thinking that on those apparently rare occasions when killers attack a large whale there is anything more than a free-for-all. It is quite unnecessary to invoke any concept of 'group feeding.'"

Its as though the science of animal behavior never came about. It has been decades since the most conservative comparative psychologists and ethologists explored in depth the questions of animal intelligence and foresight, concluding across the board that both exist in degrees throughout the animal kingdom from such relatively simple organisms as planaria and wasps to titmice and rats. The same unanimous acceptance of animal cooperation is to be found for decades among ecologists and ethologists, who early on discriminated between gregariousness, as in the schooling behavior of fish, an adaptation for protection against predators in which individuals hide themselves in groups, and true sociality in which each individual recognizes every other individual in a group and each member has a distinct role within an organized whole. Even before the advent of sociobiology, cooperative behavior in animals ranging from spiders and ants to sea lions, wolves and elephants had been thoroughly documented, and from sociobiology has come the idea that cooperation exists among animals and humans for fundamentally the same reasons. These include defense against predators, increased foraging success as in hunting big game by wolves, and competition within and between species for resources.

The Northwest Coastal Indians likened the killer whale to the wolf, calling it the wolf of the sea. Clearly, both the wolf and the orca benefit from cooperation in attacking and killing animals much larger than themselves, and social behavior helps individuals in other ways such as protection of young against predators. When wolves attack a moose, their behavior is not pell-mell, a free-for-all in which there is a mad rush of wolves flinging themselves one on top of the other at the victim, but a carefully and finely orchestrated strategy of cooperation without which individuals would incur greater risks, make fewer kills and get less food. Cooperation is no less apparent when members of a wolf pack confront a menacing grizzly, or when packs of hyenas meet at territorial boundaries, competing for real estate, or when groups of male lions make war with one another for possession of breeding territories and the females therein, or when lionesses cross-suckle kittens. And each one of these examples represents the very advantages believed to account for the evolution of cooperation or social life in humans.

Obviously, orcas are highly cooperative in attacking great whales, moreso really than wolves attacking moose or lions attacking buffalo. So impressed were the Makah whalers of the Pacific Northwest with the precision of orcas attacking large whales that they referred to them as being "one step above god," the only instance of such praise for any animal (or person), to my knowledge. In part what this indicates is that the orcas' cooperative behavior killing whales was much superior to that of the Makah's, possibly the best primitive whalers. And in part it probably stems from the fact that the Indian whalers knew that orcas had the capacity to destroy them, but they didn't despite the fact that the whalers competed with orcas for whales.

Equating the grazing behavior of fin whales to the orca's wolf-like and human-like predatory behavior on large, dangerous whales is utterly stupid, but one can only imagine that a scientist would do such a thing if he were obsessed with defending a personal dogma essentially the same as Aristotle's ladder of being with humans on top, the same homocentric ideology espoused by western civilization up through Descartes into this century. Or, perhaps, having made his professional career on the basis of studies dependent on the whaling industry, Matthews is resisting the inevitable death of whaling. For his sake, let us hope that he is not resisting the recent consensus of cetaceans as intelligent, aware beings out of what could be remorse and guilt were he to accept it. Another internationally known marine mammalogist of Matthews' generation, Vic Scheffer, killed thousands of sea lions for study in his career, but, after retiring, as much as admonished his earlier values in A Voice for Wildlife, which recognizes animals as something more than manageable resources.

Not Matthews. Though he describes the remarkable capacity of delphinids to imitate other species, cetaceans, humans and so on, which they learn to do with incredible speed and perfection, often spontaneously, he would reverse the implications:

"Although the brain of the cetaceans is large and shows a complexity of development of the cerebral cortex, there is no reason for supposing that the cetacean capacity for learning is associated with intelligence."

In one full sweep, Matthews overturns the consistent evidence from neurophysiology, physiological and comparative psychology, and experimental psychology that brain development generally correlates with learning and intelligence.

In so doing he does not offer one reason why we should agree with his proposition, to my knowledge unique among scientists of our time. And he fails to mention the experimental studies of dolphin learning which generally equate their intelligence to humanity's. Neither does he let the reader know that in fact the cerebral cortex of some dolphin species is more complex than that of the human brain. It's quite amusing in one sense, tragically sad in another, that modern science pointed to the human brain as the pinnacle of evolution until John

Lilly made it widely known that dolphin brains are more highly developed. Since then we've heard less and less in the biology and anthropology books about the long-touted ladder of perfection with man and his gloriously convoluted brain on top.

Because science is our culture, a culture of which the everyday man is ignorant, and, often, I think, in conflict between a sense of awe on one hand and resentment on the other, it is crucial that the gap between professional science and the rest of society be bridged. It is up to scientists to build the bridge, to make the work of science accessible to the non-scientists, and to participate as lay ministers whose function it is to translate the heart-felt reason (prayers) of the congregation to the high priesthood of science, and the priestly magic into street language. The barrier is largely one of language: in fact, science is nothing magical, and the knowledge of science exists for the most part in common knowledge ranging from ancient wisdom and religious books to fairy tales, poetry, novels and stories. The famous dolphins of ancient Greece who befriended children were not labelled as neurotics, the Greek fishermen who interacted with dolphins daily thought of them as sacred and intelligent for good reason—the dolphins led them to fish and also guided them home when they were lost or imperilled by stormy seas. And whatever else Aristotle contributed to the justification of our egocentrism, he did mention that dolphins have a language, albeit not Greek, he said, judging by the accent.

Matthews' book reflects the culmination of western hubris, what Ortega y Gasset termed pious idealism or intellectualism, and what an Indian raised in the white man's way meant when he commented that he learned that a man thinks with his head and not his heart. When we worship ideas because what we (think we) know serves us well, when intellectual knowledge is the common yardstick of a society, the means to fame and fortune, then humans become brainy egos fragmented within themselves, from one another, from other beings and the world, everything in fact but their self-serving beliefs. True intelligence is possible not because of intellect, ideas, schooling or mental "training," but only when the intellectual faculty is a tool in service to the whole being. Knowledge, wisdom and genuine intelligence are not the province or the content of ego or consciousness, but possible only when we are unconscious of ourselves, when there is no thought, no past, no idea, no projection, that is when we are transparent, susceptible to truth, absorptive, alert, knowing and keenly alive. When the self is still, we can see the intelligence of the dolphin, communicate with the orca, and receive the gift of highest reason, intuition, that which is present to us in the absence of ego-thought processes. THAT is true intelligence, and with it at the fore, intellect may be called upon in the service of virtue—right thought and action.

But the intelligence of Matthews is not our intelligence, and the difference can be ascribed only to professionalism, individuals fearing possibilities borne of fearless perception, which, if accepted by others may jeopardize their status, success, fame and material security. The majority of cetologists like the majority of biologists and other scientists locked into the Cartesian-Newtonian mode, more or less conform with Matthews' perception of cetacean sociality, communication and intelligence. Many secretly believe that cetaceans are advanced species, but the split between their private and professional views is symptomatic of a society burdened with fear and so obsessed by competition for social esteem that accurate observation, clear thought, effective cooperation and solution of real problems are largely inhibited.

A few intrepid professionals together with many amateurs, unhindered by desire for professional gain or fear of losing professional status, are changing cetology and helping to bring about the human/earth benefits of this age of the whale. Understanding cetaceans promises to help us understand and change ourselves, the most pressing need for us and them.

I am no longer angry at Matthews, and it was a challenging personal voyage for me to move beyond my own egotistical

Beaky, wild but friendly dolphin, often towed boats and children
in southern England.

attachments to the destiny of whales: My desire that other
humans would revel in the light of whales, come to the awareness, delight and fascination I had known with them; and, fear
that other humans would go on destroying these angels of the
sea. My criticisms of Matthews' book no longer apply to him,
and I trust even now in the ultimate destiny of his soul, just as
I trust in infinite, eternal love to prevail. After all, you see, that
was my real lesson from the whales: love thy brother more than
thy life. There is nothing to lose, nothing to fear. We are Spirit.
"And the Spirit was made flesh."

24

The Dogon and
the Nommo

THE SIRIUS MYSTERY will become known as one of the most important books of our time. Robert Temple meticulously wrote a scholarly book which convinces the most left-brained person that dolphins may come from outer space. The book is about the mythology of the Dogon, a pastoral people of northern Africa.

Prior to the discovery of Sirius B, an invisible star associated with Sirius A, the Dog Star, the Dogon had told western scientists that it exists. They had explained that the dark star has a revolutionary period around the light star of 50 years. Later when astronomical observation first observed a wobble in Sirius A, indicating a dark twin star orbiting with it, western scientists returned to the Dogon to ask how they knew about the dark star.

The Dogon's most important story was etched hundreds of years ago in their cave of records. They showed the old drawings of the light and dark star orbiting through space, and they explained that the information about Sirius A and B was given to them by creatures who came from that part of the cosmos.

"A Team," Orca Project volunteers, leaving Cracroft Island camp, 1983.

These creatures resembled dolphins, called Nommo by the Dogon. The Nommo arrived in a spaceship which sent a 3-pronged landing craft down to earth. The pod landed and used a strong current of air to hollow a place beneath the craft. Then water was squirted into the hollow and the Nommo dropped into the water and began to teach the Dogon about who they were and from where they came.

The Nommo said that they are from the third planet out in the Sirius system. Their planet was described as similar to earth but with a greater portion covered with seas. The Nommo told the Dogon that their planetary races include the dolphins of our seas as well as humans who were described as the trouble makers.

The astronomers determined the revolutionary period of Sirius B around Sirius A to be 50.1 years, which further substantiates the incredible accuracy of the Dogon mythology. The Dogon also knew the number of moons around Jupiter though they had no way of observing them from earth.

Sirius has been far more important in the history of earth than most of us could imagine. Temple shows that the Egyptians set their calendar by the rising of Sirius before the sun on July 23rd, an important date among other cultures as well. And ancient art and mythology abound with renditions and stories of dolphin-like beings who taught humans astronomy, mathematics, and cosmology. The Babylonians and Scandinavians are examples as well as the descendents of the Inca who claim that a spacecraft visited Lake Titikaka from which came dolphin-beings who taught their ancestors. A similar mythology exists in the Malaysian archipelago.

The new age is the revival of ancient wisdom that has been held by the aboriginal peoples of earth. That wisdom is surfacing in dream, writing, art and film. Like the Dogon of North Africa, the aboriginal peoples of North America trace their sacred wisdom back to Star People, extra-terrestrials who gave them the chanupa, the sacred pipe. All across this land the many native societies have a common expression which translates as "all my relations." It means that I am related to all things or all things are my relatives. All forms of life are related and deserve to sit in the sacred circle of life.

The real work of whale watching is a meeting of nations.

25

The Emerging Philosophy

THE EMERGING PHILOSOPHY WAS REBORN with the men who caste it; they include Aldo Leopold, the father of the land ethic, Albert Einstein, whose relativity made time dependent upon space, Carl Jung whose psychology placed the conscious mind in an inexorable relationship to the unconscious, Picasso whose cubism spoke of wholeness and sacred geometry and whose primal art pulled us back to our connection with the animals and the earth, and the prototypical man of that seminal generation of the 1880's, Jose Ortego y Gasset whose philosophy of co-existence of ego and circumstance slayed the bull of Cartesian idealism once and for all.

Upon their shoulders we now stand at the edge of a new age. Interdependence is the key word for this new age; it is the return of the ancient wisdom of the interdependence of all life. An age of empowerment, the return of mythology and the gods, an age in which masculine transcendence and feminine immanence stand together, an epoch of expanding awareness of the multi-dimensional nature of reality, and most important our TAKING responsibility for our lives. With that responsibility comes the deep ethical sense that we also are responsible for our home and one another—not co-dependence but interdependence in the sense that "no one is crucified alone, no one gets to heaven alone."

The lover's quarrel I conducted with mechanistic thinking represents the crisis of our age. It is a crisis because we find ourselves afloat without a rudder. The very foundation of our culture is in doubt; it no longer offers us a way into safe harbor. Essentially we are between philosophies. Our most fundamental assumptions about reality are uncertain.

It all began, ostensibly, with the Heisenberg Principle in physics in the early part of the twentieth century. Dubbed the Principle of Uncertainty, it meant that we could not be certain whether the smallest atomic phenomenon is a wave or a particle. It all depended on the experiment and the observer, which meant that we could not be certain any longer about the nature of reality. It meant, in short, that our knowledge no longer was certain, that it was dependent.

Prior to that time western civilization was seduced by its own vanity which rested squarely upon the certainty of Newtonian physics, the view that the universe is mechanistic and thus mathematically predictable. That was the heart of western culture. Mechanistic science was our mythology.

Few of us today understand the meaning of mythology, much less the pervasiveness of science as "the great myth of western man" as Ortega said. If you want to know the mythology of a people all you need to do is ask them where their babies come from. Their answer indicates their primary way of thinking about themselves and their world. The vast majority of people in the world today will answer with a story about a sperm and egg uniting to form an embryo, and so on. Their story is the story of science.

Very few have observed sperm cells or ova and even fewer have observed them unite to form an embryo which develops into a fetus. Yet, almost all absolutely insist that the story is true. Just as they are apt to insist that atoms and electrons really exist. How many would believe that not one person in the history of the world has ever seen an atom? Mythology indeed.

Science is the way of thinking that thinks us. It is our story about where we come from and who and what we are. Because it became uncertain of its principles, its assumptions, the entire world is in a state of crisis now. Is knowledge contingent? Is it dependent upon the knower? Do we determine reality by our thoughts, beliefs and convictions? Who is in charge anyway?

The most important concept I encountered in 15 years of university education was the placebo effect. I must give a close second to the idea of self-fulfilling prophesy. The placebo effect means that our beliefs hold power, not the things in the world. Sugar pills heal people because we believe in their power. We give them power. Which means the power really belongs to us, not to some chemical agent. Which in turn means that the mind is the most powerful thing there is.

To take it further, the placebo effect means that our experience of reality is dictated by our beliefs in reality. If we are convinced that cancer is deadly and a doctor tells us we have it, there is a very high probability that we will die. And I am convinced that is why many people do die. They kill themselves with their beliefs.

The mechanistic view of reality had us believing that we are helpless, that we are simply effects of so many different causes. Our absolute belief in that view generated a self-fulfilling prophesy. We believed we are effects or victims and our beliefs were powerful enough to create victim reality thus perpetuating the myth. The mechanistic mythology disempowered humanity. It held us in fear, destroyed our health, spawned materialism and greed, and reinforced separatism and egoism to the brink of global annihilation. Beliefs are powerful causes.

The truth is that we are causes, not effects. That's what the placebo effect complies. That's what the Uncertainty Principle of physics also indicates. And that is the heart of the emerging philosophy. It also is what the Bible means when it speaks of us being created in the likeness (not image) of God. The likeness refers to creative mind and eternal life. What will emerge from the present revolution in thought is the recognition that "we create our own reality." Which already is a widespread expression indicative of the new mythology. What has not fully emerged as yet is the realization that we are responsible for what we think, what we feel, and everything that happens to us. Everything. We reap what we sow.

The world government is experiencing its own crisis because we may escape their efforts to control us. And they are no friends of the whale.

All around the world it was common for societies to initiate their young people into the mysteries. The form of initiation has varied a lot, ranging from deprivation to meditation and hallucinogenic drugs. All for one purpose: to show that there is more to reality than meets the eye. . .that there is more than the body. We discover that what we are is not limited to the body. We discover that the body does not contain us and that we are limitless. Out-of-body experiences change a person's life. He discovers that his true nature is nothing less than infinite and eternal. He finds out that the Bible is correct: we are created in the likeness of God. Which means that we are invulnerable, that death is merely the passing of a body, and that there is nothing to fear. There never was.

When all the fear is gone, as Jampolsky said, there remains only love.

In 1975, nearly twenty years ago at this writing, I died. I was sitting on a couch with a friend in Bellevue, Washington, explaining that I felt as though I kept walking up stairs at the top of which was a doorway. Each time I got to the doorway I knew the answer was on the other side but for some reason I couldn't go through. Then it happened. I was gone. I went through that door and left my body and this dimension behind me. In an eternal moment I found myself everywhere at once beyond time. I experienced all of time and space and more—total knowledge and bliss. For a while I was outside this universe observing it expand and contract like a heart. In those days only the Big Bang theory existed in western science, though the Hindus had the "long view" for thousands of years. The long view first appeared in the scientific press several years later, but I knew with absolute conviction that the universe had expanded and contracted many times, not merely once.

I went to the place known as the Great Void. I called it death because I knew that it is where we come from and to where we return, and where in fact we always are. The Bible calls my experience revelation. What was revealed was our true nature.

Normally, we are conscious only of the 3-D world. Traumas, near-death experiences, and initiations can reveal higher dimensions of which there are many. What we discover is that we exist in these higher dimensions at the same time as we exist within the 3-dimensional world. Expansion of consciousness means discovering more of ourselves. It means experiencing directly our multi-dimensional nature. When we pass beyond all dimensions we come to the Great Void or the Godhead. . .our true nature.

Such experiences make us laugh at fear and they fill our hearts with the joy that comes from the ecstasy and bliss of God. And of course they set us free of ego which allows us to love. But what has all this to do with whales?

The dolphins and whales are conscious of many dimensions simultaneously. They exist within our 3-dimensional world while they also are aware in other dimensions and the Great Void. Like us they are multi-dimensional beings, only they know it. They are here on earth by their own choice to help humanity survive and to remind us to be co-guardians of earth with them, a contract we made thousands of years ago.

The cetaceans have been working on many levels to teach us, and one of their greatest gifts is to serve as portals for us to become aware of the extent of our own being. Twenty years ago the orca whales facilitated my journey to the Great Void. They and other cetaceans are available to those of us who are ready to take the ultimate trip.

Few people have been to the Great Void but many will make the journey in the years ahead. When they return they will know with absolute certainty who and what they are, and they will elevate this world. They will know what the orcas taught me. I agreed to translate the sacred wisdom of the cetacean nations for the human family. That wisdom is simple: "Life is sacred. Honor it."

Thinking with the Heart

A native American raised in a mission said that he had learned how to eat with a fork, sleep on a bed, use a toilet, and read the Bible. He also learned "that a man thinks with his head and not his heart." We are entering the age of the heart.

As we stand around the fire on the Orca Project, I tell everyone that people are like pendulums: all the pendulums in a room may be started at different times, but three days later they all will be swinging in precise synchrony. When people hold hands in a circle it takes but a few minutes before their hearts beat as one.

It turns out that the aboriginals and poets and artists were right all along. It is possible to think with the heart. The heart has been found to secrete neurohormones which influence the brain and nervous system. The heart itself generates an electromagnetic field. One of our goals in the Orca Project was to get our volunteers within the powerful field of the orcas' hearts. When humans pass through that field it changes them. Like other cetaceans the orcas are here to activate our sacred wisdom. They have impressive brains, but they communicate with us heart to heart. They are teachers of the heart. Despite all appearances to the contrary they are our brothers. Which is why they are reluctant to harm us.

Jesus has been credited with saying that he saw the dawning of a "new age of spiritual brotherhood" on planet earth. The sun of that age has risen. Few of them can now be found, but the original symbol for Jesus was not a horizontal fish but rather a vertical dolphin.

The World University is in the sea. Its faculty are dolphins, orcas and whales. Like small children we may go there and swim with them. And they will bring us home.

Science has led us from the brain back to the heart. More beautiful in its implications the heart has been found to be entrained to...the earth. The radio-frequency of the earth, its pulsing vibratory rate, is what regulates our hearts which regulate our brains which regulate our bodies.

Even more beautiful is the discovery that a person could alter the frequency of the earth locally by holding a certain feeling in his heart. That feeling was love. Which suggests that not only does the earth speak to our hearts but that our thoughts and feelings influence the earth. *That's interdependence.* And that is why, as Lao Tzu said, if we would save the earth and the whales, we must look first to ourselves. Thinking with the heart means listening to our feelings and letting them guide us. That is the lesson of the whale people for humanity. As my native Brothers say, "Na Nin Da Hey." Let us sing from the heart.

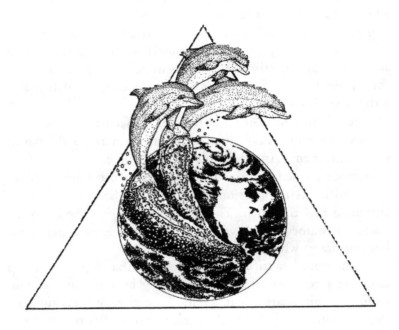

Lunara

Cloud maidens court the ocean
Silver feathers fill the heart